SUPERMAN
THE POWER WITHIN

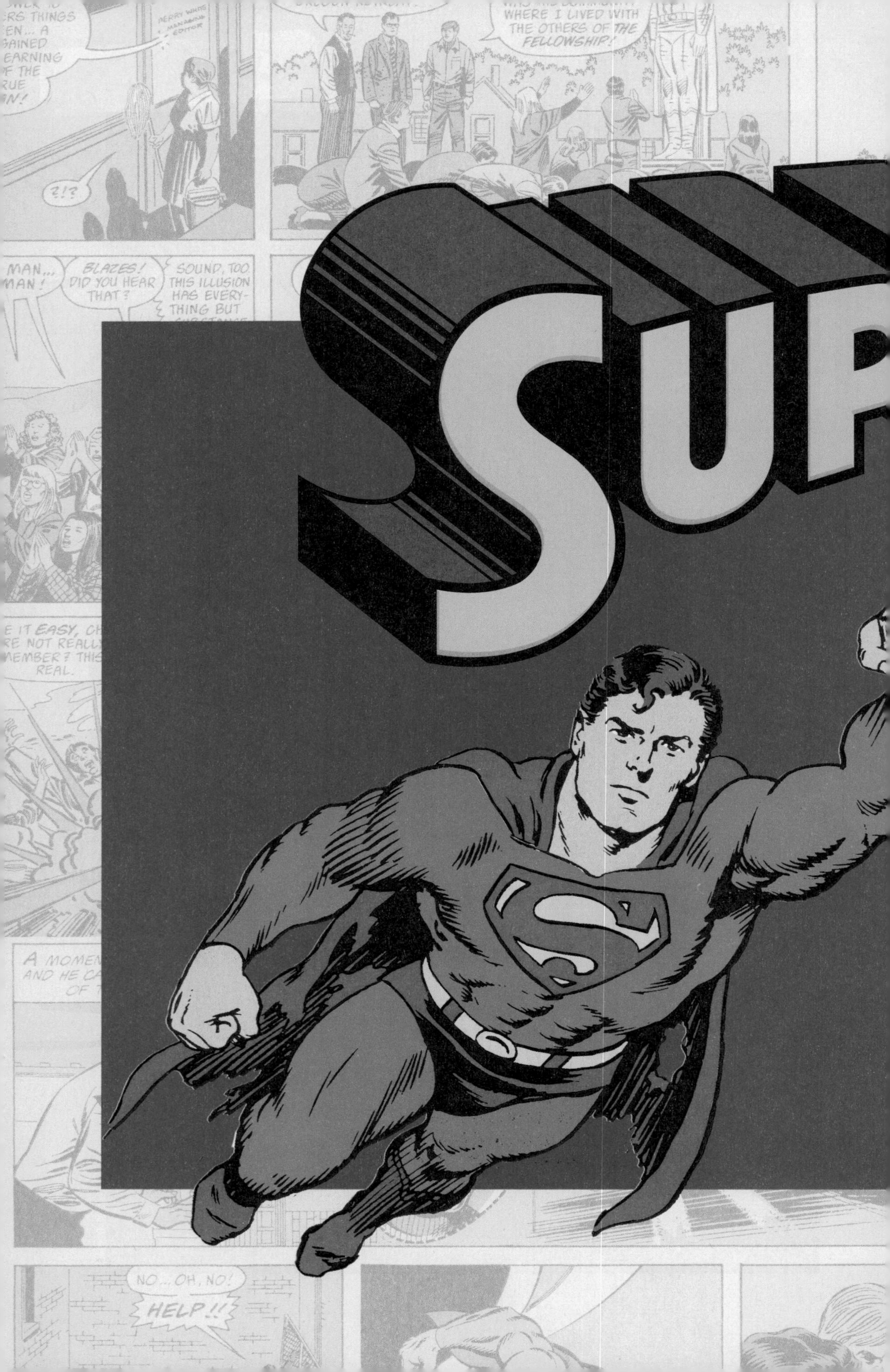
WHERE I LIVED WITH THE OTHERS OF THE FELLOWSHIP!
?!?
BLAZES! DID YOU HEAR THAT?
SOUND, TOO. THIS ILLUSION HAS EVERY- THING BUT
NO...OH, NO!
HELP!!

ERMAN

THE POWER WITHIN

Roger Stern
William Messner-Loebs
WRITERS

Curt Swan
Murphy Anderson
John Beatty
Dennis Janke
ARTISTS

Tom Ziuko
Petra Scotese
Glenn Whitmore
COLORISTS

Bill Oakley
LETTERER

Kerry Gammill
Bob McLeod
John Nyberg
Dave Gibbons
Alex Niño
Dean Motter
Brent Anderson
John Severin
Murphy Anderson
Original Series Covers

SUPERMAN created by
Jerry Siegel and **Joe Shuster**
By Special Arrangement with the
Jerry Siegel Family

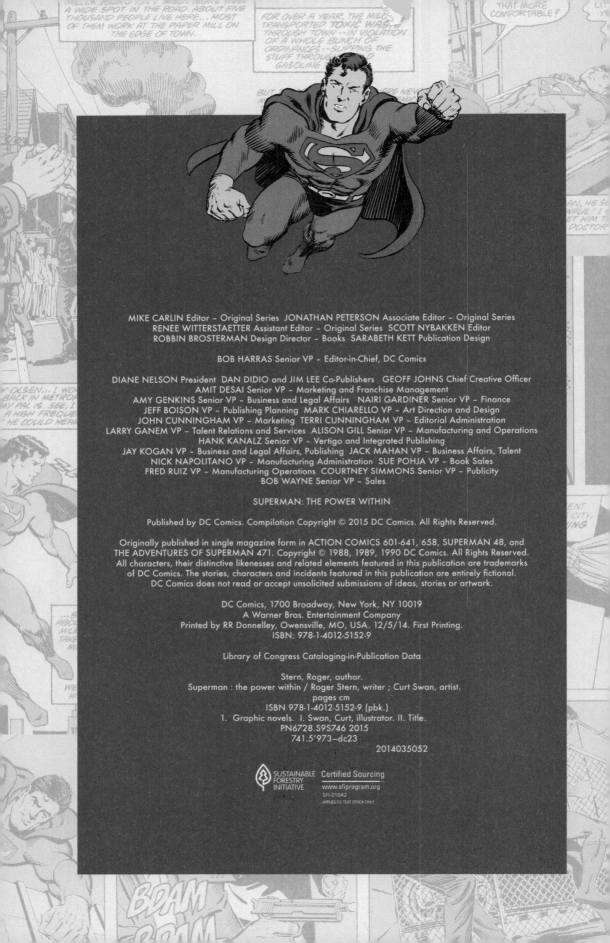

MIKE CARLIN Editor – Original Series JONATHAN PETERSON Associate Editor – Original Series
RENEE WITTERSTAETTER Assistant Editor – Original Series SCOTT NYBAKKEN Editor
ROBBIN BROSTERMAN Design Director – Books SARABETH KETT Publication Design

BOB HARRAS Senior VP – Editor-in-Chief, DC Comics

DIANE NELSON President DAN DIDIO and JIM LEE Co-Publishers GEOFF JOHNS Chief Creative Officer
AMIT DESAI Senior VP – Marketing and Franchise Management
AMY GENKINS Senior VP – Business and Legal Affairs NAIRI GARDINER Senior VP – Finance
JEFF BOISON VP – Publishing Planning MARK CHIARELLO VP – Art Direction and Design
JOHN CUNNINGHAM VP – Marketing TERRI CUNNINGHAM VP – Editorial Administration
LARRY GANEM VP – Talent Relations and Services ALISON GILL Senior VP – Manufacturing and Operations
HANK KANALZ Senior VP – Vertigo and Integrated Publishing
JAY KOGAN VP – Business and Legal Affairs, Publishing JACK MAHAN VP – Business Affairs, Talent
NICK NAPOLITANO VP – Manufacturing Administration SUE POHJA VP – Book Sales
FRED RUIZ VP – Manufacturing Operations COURTNEY SIMMONS Senior VP – Publicity
BOB WAYNE Senior VP – Sales

SUPERMAN: THE POWER WITHIN

Published by DC Comics. Compilation Copyright © 2015 DC Comics. All Rights Reserved.

Originally published in single magazine form in ACTION COMICS 601-641, 658, SUPERMAN 48, and
THE ADVENTURES OF SUPERMAN 471. Copyright © 1988, 1989, 1990 DC Comics. All Rights Reserved.
All characters, their distinctive likenesses and related elements featured in this publication are trademarks
of DC Comics. The stories, characters and incidents featured in this publication are entirely fictional.
DC Comics does not read or accept unsolicited submissions of ideas, stories or artwork.

DC Comics, 1700 Broadway, New York, NY 10019
A Warner Bros. Entertainment Company
Printed by RR Donnelley, Owensville, MO, USA. 12/5/14. First Printing.
ISBN: 978-1-4012-5152-9

Library of Congress Cataloging-in-Publication Data

Stern, Roger, author.
Superman : the power within / Roger Stern, writer ; Curt Swan, artist.
pages cm
ISBN 978-1-4012-5152-9 (pbk.)
1. Graphic novels. I. Swan, Curt, illustrator. II. Title.
PN6728.S9S746 2015
741.5'973—dc23
2014035052

SUSTAINABLE
FORESTRY
INITIATIVE

Certified Sourcing
www.sfiprogram.org
SFI-01042
APPLIES TO TEXT STOCK ONLY

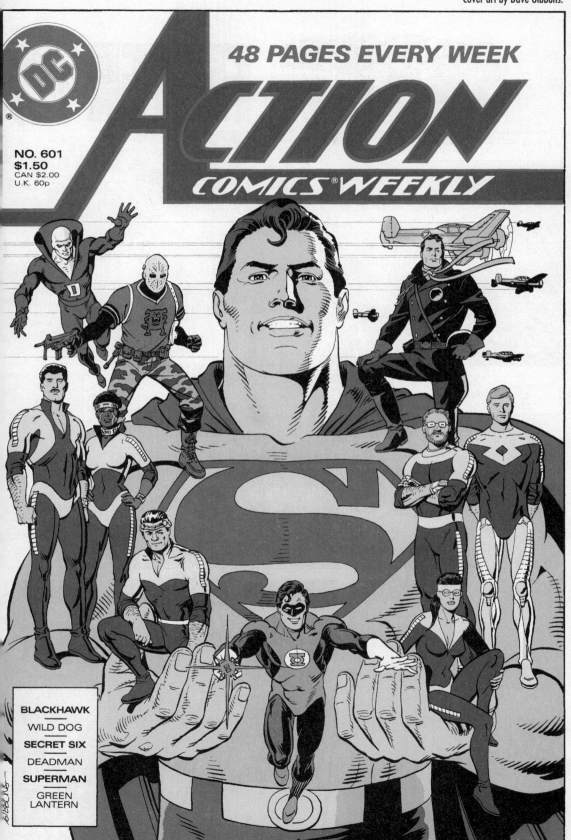

Cover art by Dave Gibbons.

48 PAGES EVERY WEEK

Action Comics Weekly

NO. 601
$1.50
CAN $2.00
U.K. 60p

BLACKHAWK

WILD DOG

SECRET SIX

DEADMAN

SUPERMAN

GREEN LANTERN

SUPERMAN®

Created by
JERRY SIEGEL &
JOE SHUSTER

FASTER THA...

THIS IS **METROPOLIS**. ELEVEN MILLION PEOPLE CALL IT HOME...

...AND AMONG THEM LIVES AND WORKS **ONE MAN** WHO IS UNLIKE ANY OTHER.

I LOVE IT UP HERE!

THAT MAN IS REPORTER **CLARK KENT**...

THERE'S NOTHING IN THE WORLD QUITE LIKE THE CITY AT THE END OF A BUSY DAY...THE SIGHTS... THE **SOUNDS**...

FOR KENT, IT TAKES BUT A MOMENT'S CONCENTRA- TION--

A MOMENT'S CONCENTRATION, AND HE CAN SEE TO THE ENDS OF THE EARTH!

SOMEBODY... ANYBODY... **HELP!**

LOCATING THE TROUBLE TAKES LESS THAN A SECOND.

NO...OH, NO! **HELP!!**

GO AHEAD, YELL YOUR **LUNGS** OUT! NOBODY CAN HEAR YA OUT HERE--

--YOU'RE MILES AWAY FROM ANYBODY THAT COULD HELP YA!

BDAM

BDAM

SPEEDING BULLET!

ROGER STERN– WRITER
CURT SWAN– PENCILLER
JOHN BEATTY– INKER
BILL OAKLEY– LETTERER
TOM ZIUKO– COLORIST
MIKE CARLIN– EDITOR

--AND ALL THE SOUNDS OF THE CITY ARE HIS TO HEAR!

MOMMY! DADDY, MOMMY'S HOME!

HEY, YA WANNA MOVE THAT THING?

...THEY'RE A MODERN STONE-AGE FAM-IL-LEE!

DOWN THAT STREET AND THREE BLOCKS TO THE RIGHT!

...AN' THEN HE SAYS, "I WAS TALKIN' TO THE DUCK!"

HELP! THEY'RE GOING TO KILL ME!

AND WHEN CLARK KENT SEES TROUBLE IN HIS CITY, HE DOES SOMETHING ABOUT IT!

I'D SAY YOU'RE WRONG.

OMIGOD.

SUPERMAN!

CONTINUED NEXT WEEK!

7

SUPERMAN "THEY CAN RUN

Created by
JERRY SIEGEL &
JOE SHUSTER

SEEING A LIFE THREATENED AT A *METROPOLIS* RAILYARD, THE *MAN OF STEEL* HAS FLOWN TO THE RESCUE...

GIVE UP?

NO...SOMEHOW, I DIDN'T *THINK* THEY WOULD. EITHER THEY'RE NEW IN TOWN, OR THEY'RE JUST NOT VERY BRIGHT. OH, WELL...

"...THEY WON'T GET FAR!"

WHAT'RE YOU *DOIN'*? WE'VE ALREADY LOST CHARLIE...AN' IF YOU DON'T SLOW DOWN, WE'LL LOSE DAVE, TOO!

SLOW DOWN? ARE YOU *MAD*?! THAT WAS *SUPERMAN* BACK THERE...

THOSE LOUSY #%$!! IF I GET OUTTA THIS ALIVE, I *SWEAR* I'LL--!

?!?

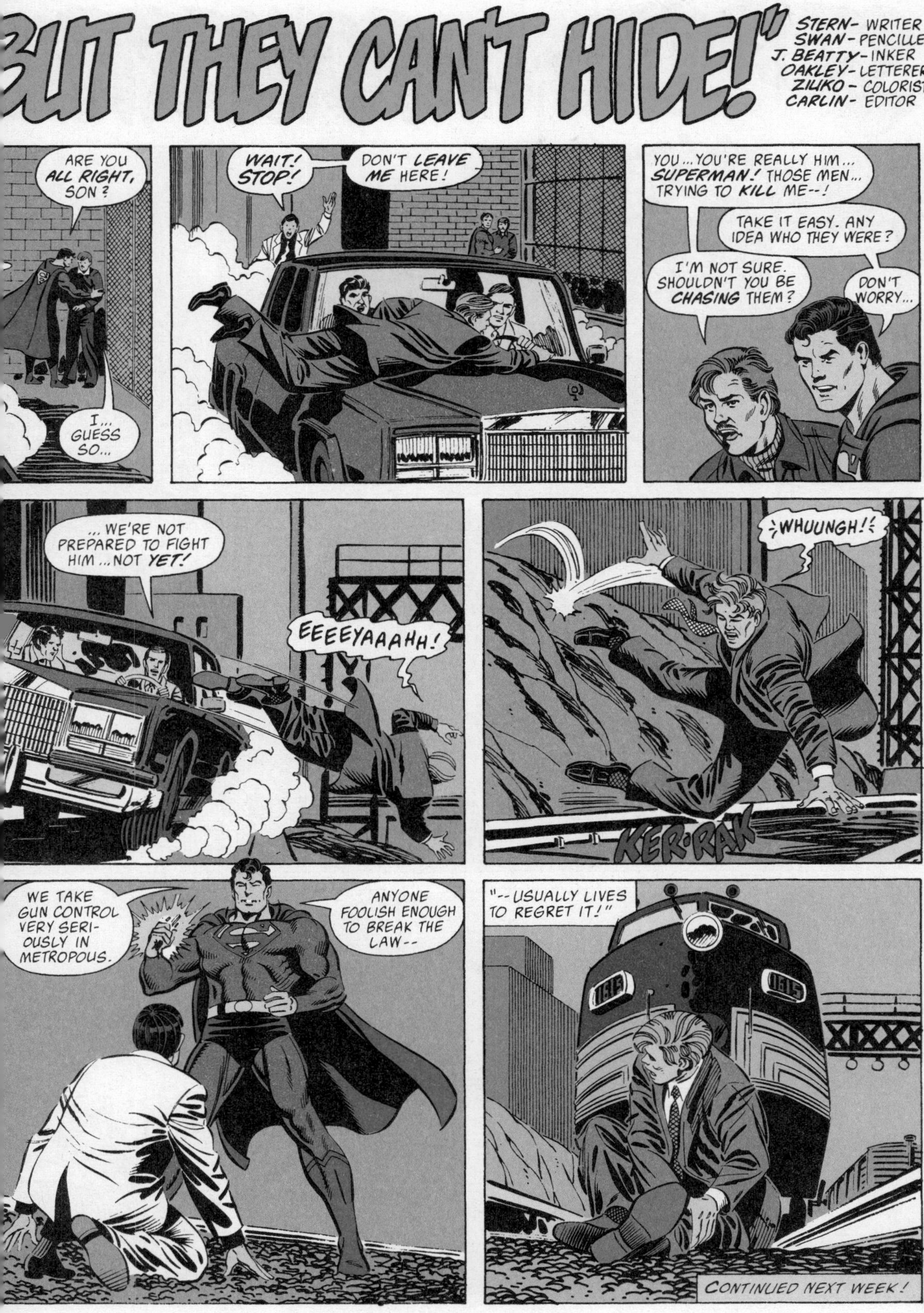
"BUT THEY CAN'T HIDE!"
STERN- WRITER
SWAN- PENCILLER
J. BEATTY- INKER
OAKLEY- LETTERER
ZILKO- COLORIST
CARLIN- EDITOR
ARE YOU ALL RIGHT, SON?
I... GUESS SO...
WAIT! STOP!
DON'T LEAVE ME HERE!
YOU... YOU'RE REALLY HIM... SUPERMAN! THOSE MEN... TRYING TO KILL ME--!
TAKE IT EASY. ANY IDEA WHO THEY WERE?
I'M NOT SURE. SHOULDN'T YOU BE CHASING THEM?
DON'T WORRY...
... WE'RE NOT PREPARED TO FIGHT HIM... NOT YET!
EEEEYAAAHH!
WHUUNGH!
KER-RAK
WE TAKE GUN CONTROL VERY SERIOUSLY IN METROPOUS.
ANYONE FOOLISH ENOUGH TO BREAK THE LAW--
"--USUALLY LIVES TO REGRET IT!"
CONTINUED NEXT WEEK!

SUPERMAN®

Created by
*JERRY SIEGEL &
JOE SHUSTER*

"MORE POWERFUL

LEG... ALL *BUSTED UP.* NO WAY OUTTA THIS ONE.

WHILE TRYING TO ESCAPE FROM SUPERMAN, A HIRED GUNMAN HAS BEEN THROWN FROM A GETAWAY CAR ...AND INTO A DEADLY SITUATION!

UGLY DAMN WAY TO--

THIS MAN'S LEG IS BROKEN... HE SHOULDN'T GIVE YOU MUCH TROUBLE! I LEFT ONE OF HIS *PARTNERS* TIED UP A QUARTER-MILE WEST OF HERE. THE POLICE WILL WANT TO TALK TO THEM *BOTH.*

GREAT DAY IN THE MORNIN'!

YOU MUST EXCUSE ME ...

"... A FRIEND OF THEIRS IS STILL *AT LARGE!* "

YOU SAID THIS'D BE A SIMPLE HIT-- YOU NEVER TOLD US THAT WE'D BE RUNNIN' UP AGAINST SUPERMAN!

THAT WAS NOT IN MY PLANS. IT SEEMS--

AT THAT MOMENT, THOUSANDS OF FEET OVER-HEAD...

THAT'S THE CAR, AND... *WHAT?!*

NAN A LOCOMOTIVE!"

ROGER STERN – WRITER
CURT SWAN – PENCILLER
JOHN BEATTY – INKER
BILL OAKLEY – LETTERER
PETRA SCOTESE – COLORIST
MIKE CARLIN – EDITOR

--DIE?

SCREEEEE

RUMMMBLLE!

HOLEE--!

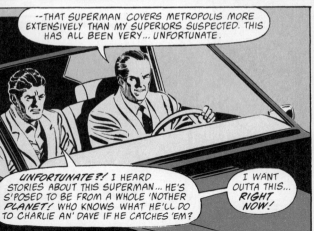

--THAT SUPERMAN COVERS METROPOLIS MORE EXTENSIVELY THAN MY SUPERIORS SUSPECTED. THIS HAS ALL BEEN VERY... UNFORTUNATE.

UNFORTUNATE?! I HEARD STORIES ABOUT THIS SUPERMAN... HE'S S'POSED TO BE FROM A WHOLE 'NOTHER PLANET! WHO KNOWS WHAT HE'LL DO TO CHARLIE AN' DAVE IF HE CATCHES 'EM?

I WANT OUTTA THIS... RIGHT NOW!

HAPPY TO OBLIGE!

B'OOM

MY GOD, WHAT WAS HE SHOT WITH?

DEATH MUST HAVE BEEN INSTANTANEOUS.

WHOEVER DID THIS WILL PAY. I SWEAR... THEY WILL PAY!

CONTINUED NEXT WEEK!

SUPERMAN®

Created by
JERRY SIEGEL &
JOE SHUSTER

"FINAL

IN PURSUING THE LAST OF A TRIO OF GUNMEN, THE MAN OF STEEL HAS DISCOVERED HIS QUARRY'S BODY, DUMPED BY THE SIDE OF THE ROAD...

WHOEVER KILLED HIM CAN'T HAVE GOTTEN FAR...THEY WON'T ESCAPE ME!

DIDJA SEE THE LOOK O SUPERMAN'S FACE?

...ATTRACTING ...ATTENTION.

NO! OH ...NO!!

I DON'T LIKE LAW-BREAKERS IN GENERAL-- ESPECIALLY IN MY TOWN--

--BUT I HAVE A PARTICULAR DIS-TASTE FOR KILLERS! DON'T MAKE ME DO SOMETHING I'LL REGRET!

ESCAPE?"

ROGER STERN – WRITER
CURT SWAN – PENCILLER
JOHN BEATTY – INKER
BILL OAKLEY – LETTERER
TOM ZIUKO – COLORER
MIKE CARLIN – EDITOR

YEAH. I WONDER WHO HE'S AFTER?

I DUNNO-- BUT I WOULDN'T WANT TO BE IN THAT GUY'S SHOES!

SEVERAL MILES AWAY...

IT'S ALL FALLING APART. I DON'T UNDERSTAND... THIS SHOULD HAVE BEEN SUCH A SIMPLE OPERATION...

...ALL WE HAD TO DO WAS INTERCEPT AND ELIMINATE ONE OF *THE FELLOWSHIP'S* IDIOT COURIERS BEFORE HE COULD DELIVER HIS MESSAGE.

I NEVER SHOULD HAVE HIRED COMMON CRIMINALS -- I SHOULD HAVE DONE THE JOB MYSELF... ALONE! I'M SURE I COULD HAVE DONE IT WITHOUT...

KRAANG

I MUSTN'T BE ARRESTED. MY SUPERIORS MUST NOT BE COMPROMISED!

ONLY ONE ALTERNATIVE--!

CONTINUED NEXT WEEK!

SUPERMAN

Created by
JERRY SIEGEL &
JOE SHUSTER

"AFTER

ON THE INTERSTATE BELTWAY OUTSIDE METROPOLIS...

BOOM

FORGET THAT LICENSE CHECK... I HAVE A CODE 11! EXPLOSION OF UNKNOWN ORIGIN JUST OFF I-995... FIVE MILES WEST OF THE BESSOLO INTERCHANGE.

WHAT COULD'VE CAUSED A BLAST LIKE THAT? A GAS TANKER?

IF THAT'S THE CASE, I HOPE THE TRUCKER GOT AWAY BEFORE IT BLEW...

WHE

WEEOOO

SUPERMAN?! HOLEE--!! WHAT'S GOING ON?

GOOD QUESTION, OFFICER...

...A FEW MINUTES AGO, I INTERRUPTED A MURDER AT THE METROPOLIS RAILYARD. TWO OF THE GUNMEN I CAPTURED. THE THIRD WAS KILLED BY THE DRIVER OF THE GETAWAY CAR AS THEY TRIED TO ESCAPE.

MOMENTS LATER...

DISPATCH REPORTS THE SURVIVING GUNMEN ARE ALREADY IN CUSTODY. SAME FOR THE GUY THEY TRIED TO--!

SUPERMAN!

SUPERMAN... YOU DID IT! YOU STOPPED THE MEN WHO WERE TRYING TO KILL ME! I OWE YOU MY LIFE! I...

MATH"

ROGER STERN – WRITER
CURT SWAN – PENCILLER
JOHN BEATTY – INKER
BILL OAKLEY – LETTERER
TOM ZIUKO – COLORIST
MIKE CARLIN – EDITOR

"...TO SURVIVE AN EXPLOSION THAT BIG, YOU'D HAVE TO BE *SUPERMAN!*"

¿UNNNGHH¿

WHAT...THE... DEVIL--?!

I RAN THE KILLER TO GROUND HERE. BUT AS I HAULED HIM OUT OF HIS CAR...SOMEHOW HE MUST HAVE TRIGGERED THAT EXPLOSION!

THIS IS ALL THAT'S LEFT.

I-I'LL NEED A STATEMENT... FOR MY REPORT.

...WHAT AM I SAYING? OF COURSE, I OWE YOU MY LIFE. WE ALL DO...THERE WAS NEVER ANY QUESTION. FORGIVE ME MY DOUBTS!

YOU ARE THE ONE, TRUE SUPERMAN! YOU ARE OUR LIGHT AND OUR WAY! THROUGH YOU, WE SHALL FIND OUR SALVATION!

WHAT?!?

CONTINUED NEXT WEEK!

SUPERMAN ® "THE TRUE

Created by
JERRY SIEGEL &
JOE SHUSTER

AFTER SAVING A YOUNG MAN'S LIFE, THE **MAN OF STEEL** HAS GARNERED AN UNUSUAL EXPRESSION OF GRATITUDE...

THIS... REALLY ISN'T NECESSARY!

I ONLY WISH TO **HONOR** YOU. WOULD YOU RATHER I DID SOMETHING ELSE?

WELL.... YOU MIGHT START WITH TELLING ME WHO YOU ARE AND WHY THREE GUNMEN WANTED TO KILL YOU. WHO WERE THEY? AND WHO MIGHT THEY HAVE BEEN WORKING WITH?

"HAVEN'T YOU HEARD HIS STORY? HIS FATHER SENT HIM TO US FROM **BEYOND THE STARS**... TO LIVE AMONG US AND SHOW US THE WAY!

"IN THE YEARS SINCE HIS COMING, HE HAS EVER USED HIS MIGHT TO BALANCE THE UNCARING FORCES OF NATURE... AND BATTLE THE EVIL OF MANKIND.

BOB...YOU CREDIT ME WITH **TOO MUCH!** YES, I HELP PEOPLE TO THE BEST OF MY ABILITIES -- BUT DESPITE ALL MY POWER, I'M **NOT** GOD.

B-BUT SUPER-MAN--!

YES, BOB... SUPER**MAN!** REMEMBER THAT!

PLEASE... GO WITH THESE POLICEMEN. THEY CAN GIVE YOU ANY HELP YOU MIGHT NEED!

SUPERMAN, NO! DON'T GO!

BELIEVER"

ROGER STERN - WRITER
CURT SWAN - PENCILLER
JOHN BEATTY - INKER
BILL OAKLEY - LETTERER
TOM ZIUKO - COLORIST
MIKE CARLIN - EDITOR

I AM *BOB GALT*, BLESSED ONE, AND I HAD NEVER SEEN THEM BEFORE. I CAN ONLY ASSUME THAT THEY WERE SENT TO END MY MISSION TO CONTACT *YOU*, OUR SAVIOR. RIGHTEOUS-NESS HAS MANY ENEMIES.

OH, BROTHER!

ARE YOU MOCKING ME?! *HEATHENS!* CAN'T YOU SEE THE HOLINESS OF THIS ONE WHO STANDS BEFORE YOU?

UH... BOB...

"HE HAS BEEN HUMANITY'S CHAMPION, ASKING NOTHING IN RETURN. HE HAS STOOD FOR *TRUTH* AND *JUSTICE*.

"WITH HIS GREAT POWERS, SO FAR BEYOND THOSE OF US MERE MORTALS, WHAT ELSE SHOULD HE BE CALLED BUT *'SAVIOR'*?"

I HAVE COME SO FAR... FACED SUCH DANGER! YOU CANNOT FORSAKE ME NOW!

PLEASE!

CONTINUED NEXT WEEK!

HIGH ABOVE DOWNTOWN METROPOLIS...

THIS HAS BEEN A FRUSTRATING AFTERNOON. AT LEAST I SAVED *BOB GALT* FROM A FATAL SHOOTING AND CAPTURED TWO OF HIS ATTACKERS. BUT THE THIRD GUNMAN WAS KILLED BY THE DRIVER OF THEIR GETAWAY CAR--

--AND WHEN I CHASED *HIM* DOWN, HE BLEW HIMSELF AND THE CAR UP! THERE'S NOT A *CLUE* TO WHO HE WAS OR WHY THEY TRIED TO KILL GALT. THERE DOESN'T SEEM TO BE ANYTHING EXTRAORDINARY ABOUT GALT--

...I'M NOT WITHOUT MY *OWN* RESOURCES.

LET'S SEE IF THE *DAILY PLANET'S* TOP INVESTIGATIVE REPORTER IS WORTHY OF HIS PAYCHECK!

SHORTLY...

I SAW THE FACE OF THE GETAWAY CAR'S DRIVER FOR ONLY A FEW SECONDS, BUT I'LL NEVER FORGET IT.

I RECALL SEEING A FACE SOMEWHAT LIKE IT IN THE *PLANET* WITHIN THE PAST YEAR...

--UNTIL...

THAT'S *HIM!*

(20)

BUT WHY WOULD THE VICE PRESIDENT OF A HIGH-TECH FIRM-- HEADQUARTERED THREE THOUSAND MILES AWAY-- BE PARTY TO A *MURDER?*

FACE ?"

ROGER STERN – WRITER
CURT SWAN – PENCILLER
JOHN BEATTY – INKER
BILL OAKLEY – LETTERER
TOM ZIUKO – COLORIST
RENÉE WITTERSTAETTER – ASSISTANT EDITOR
MIKE CARLIN – EDITOR

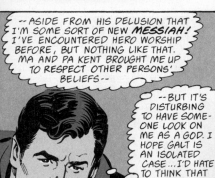

-- ASIDE FROM HIS DELUSION THAT I'M SOME SORT OF NEW *MESSIAH!* I'VE ENCOUNTERED HERO WORSHIP BEFORE, BUT NOTHING LIKE THAT. MA AND PA KENT BROUGHT ME UP TO RESPECT OTHER PERSONS' BELIEFS --

-- BUT IT'S DISTURBING TO HAVE SOMEONE LOOK ON ME AS A GOD. I HOPE GALT IS AN ISOLATED CASE... I'D HATE TO THINK THAT SOMEONE HAS STARTED THE *FIRST CHURCH OF SUPERMAN!*

I'D LEAVE THINGS TO THE POLICE TO HANDLE, BUT SOMETHING TELLS ME THERE'S A MYSTERY BEHIND THIS ATTEMPTED MURDER THAT WOULD CHALLENGE EVEN *THE BATMAN!*

I MAY NOT BE THE GREAT DETECTIVE BATMAN IS, BUT HE'S NOT INVOLVED IN THIS CASE -- *I* AM. BESIDES...

IN LESS TIME THAN IT TAKES TO TELL, *CLARK KENT* SCANS THROUGH MONTHS OF THE NEWSPAPER'S MICROFILM FILES WITH HIS AMAZING VISION POWERS --

SAY, ANNE...YOU WORK THE BUSINESS BEAT... WHAT DO YOU KNOW ABOUT A FELLOW NAMED CHARLES CULPEPPER?

ACCIDENT?

CULPEPPER? NOT MUCH... HE'S SUPPOSED TO BE A REAL UP-AND-COMER ... AT LEAST HE *WAS*, UNTIL THIS AFTERNOON'S ACCIDENT.

YEAH, THE NEWS JUST CAME OVER THE WIRE. HE WAS BADLY BURNED IN AN ELECTRICAL FIRE OUT ON THE COAST... *LESS THAN AN HOUR AGO!*

?!?!?!

CONTINUED NEXT WEEK!

SUPERMAN

Created by
JERRY SIEGEL &
JOE SHUSTER

"Questions

THE CITY ROOM OF THE METROPOLIS DAILY PLANET...

IS THE STORY ON THE CULPEPPER ACCIDENT IN THIS WIRE COPY?

WHU--? Y-YEAH, *MR. KENT*... TH-THERE'S EVEN A PHOTO.

GEEZ! WHAT'S HIS HURRY?

HMM... THAT'S EITHER CULPEPPER OR A VERY GOOD DOUBLE ON THE STRETCHER. BUT THE TIME OF HIS ACCIDENT, ACCORDING TO THIS, IS WITHIN SECONDS--

AT THAT MOMENT, ON THE GROUNDS OF A CALIFORNIA BURN CENTER...

WHAT IN BLAZES IS GOING ON, *JACOBS*? WHY DID I HAVE TO HEAR ABOUT THIS ACCIDENT ON THE RADIO?

SORRY, *MR. HODGES*... IT WAS ALL MOST UNEXPECTED. WE HAD TO SCRAMBLE TO COME UP WITH A CONVINCING *COVER STORY!*

I SEE. OUR ORGANIZATION WASN'T COMPROMISED, I HOPE!

NO, SIR! BUT I'M AFRAID WE FAILED TO TERMINATE THE COURIER.

"...THE METROPOLIS POLICE HAVE HIM IN CUSTODY FOR QUESTIONING."

YOUR ASSAILANTS WERE *HIRED* TO KILL YOU, MR. GALT... THEY DON'T KNOW ANYTHING ABOUT WHO HIRED THEM. I'LL ASK YOU AGAIN... WHO WOULD WANT TO KILL YOU?

I ALREADY TOLD YOU... *NON-BELIEVERS* MUST HAVE BEEN BEHIND THE ATTACK!

UH-HUH. AND WHO ARE THESE NON-BELIEVERS?

THEY LURK IN SHADOWS AND REVILE OUR LORD SUPERMAN. THEY HAVE TRIED TO KEEP ME FROM HIS BLESSED PRESENCE!

ᴬᴺᴰ Mysteries"

ROGER STERN - WRITER
CURT SWAN - PENCILLER
JOHN BEATTY - INKER
BILL OAKLEY - LETTERER
TOM ZIUKO - COLORIST
RENEE WITTERSTAETTER - ASSISTANT EDITOR
MIKE CARLIN - EDITOR

--OF MY CATCHING HIM ON THE OUTSKIRTS OF METROPOLIS. HE WAS INVOLVED IN TRYING TO KILL ONE MAN AND HAD JUST KILLED ANOTHER. AND WHEN I GRABBED HIM HE BLEW HIMSELF UP...

...OR SO I THOUGHT! THIS WIRE STORY PUTS HIM THREE THOUSAND MILES AWAY... SERIOUSLY INJURED BY AN ELECTRICAL FIRE.

PERHAPS I CAUGHT A DIFFERENT MAN? NO, I'M GETTING A LITTLE TOO OLD TO BELIEVE IN EVIL TWINS. SOMETHING STRANGE IS GOING ON HERE... AND SUPERMAN IS GOING TO GET TO THE BOTTOM OF IT!

CULPEPPER WAS ACTUALLY CAPTURED BY... BY SUPERMAN! HE RESORTED TO THE MASS TELEPORTER TO ESCAPE, BUT AS YOU KNOW IT'S STILL QUITE EXPERIMENTAL AND...

I KNOW, YOU IDIOT--

--LOWER YOUR VOICE! THIS IS SERIOUS... I HADN'T PLANNED ON A DIRECT CONFRONTATION WITH SUPERMAN FOR MONTHS! HE MUSTN'T LEARN ABOUT US YET. WHAT'S THE STATUS OF THE COURIER?

AS FAR AS WE CAN TELL--

YEAH, RIGHT. MR. GALT, WE HAVE SOME NICE DOCTORS THAT WE'D LIKE YOU TO SEE...

JUST A MINUTE, DETECTIVE! I'M VERY INTERESTED IN HEARING WHAT THIS MAN HAS TO SAY!

WHO--?

CONTINUED NEXT WEEK!

SUPERMAN

Created by
JERRY SIEGEL &
JOE SHUSTER

"AND THERE

AN INTERROGATION AT A METROPOLIS PRECINCT HOUSE HAS JUST COME TO AN END WHEN...

IF YOU'RE FINISHED WITH HIM, *I'D* LIKE TO TALK TO BOB GALT.

WHAT'S HE TO *YOU*, MISTER--?

KENT! I THINK MY READERS MIGHT WANT TO HEAR HIS STORY!

CLARK KENT... GEEZ, I'M A BIG FAN O' YOURS! YOUR COLUMN IS THE FIRST THING I READ IN THE *DAILY PLANET...* UH, AFTER THE COMICS AND THE SPORTS PAGE.

YES, WELL, SUPERMAN IS A BUSY FELLOW. TELL ME, DO YOU KNOW *THIS MAN?*

NO. WHY?

I HAVE NO PROOF, BUT I BELIEVE HE HIRED THE MEN WHO TRIED TO KILL YOU. HE WORKS FOR A COMPANY CALLED *SEQUOIA TECH-TRONICS...* DOES THAT RING ANY BELLS?

NO, *NO!* LOOK, I TOLD THE POLICE ALL I COULD, AND THEY THOUGHT I WAS *CRAZY!*

THE WAY I HEARD IT, YOU TREATED SUPERMAN AS IF HE WERE THE *SECOND COMING.* WHAT'S THE STORY ON THAT?

HMM... I HATE TO TAKE ADVANTAGE OF THE MAN'S BELIEFS, HOWEVER MISGUIDED THEY MAY BE... BUT I MUST GET HIM TO OPEN UP!

WILL BE A SIGN!"

ROGER STERN- WRITER
CURT SWAN- PENCILLER
JOHN BEATTY- INKER
BILL OAKLEY- LETTERER
TOM ZIUKO- COLORIST
MIKE CARLIN- EDITOR

THERE'S NO PROBLEM WITH MY TALKING TO GALT, IS THERE? HE'S NOT CHARGED WITH ANYTHING?

NO, BUT HE SEEMS A LITTLE *DINGY.* WE WERE GOING TO SHIP HIM OVER TO THE SHRINKS--!

SURELY THAT'S NOT NECESSARY? HOW ABOUT IF I VOUCH FOR HIM?

SOON...

SO, BOB, I HEAR YOU'VE HAD QUITE A DAY IN OUR CITY... *GUNMEN* TRYING TO SHOOT YOU... *SUPERMAN* COMING TO YOUR RESCUE!

I CAME HERE TO FIND SUPERMAN... BUT HE LEFT ME ONCE I WAS SAFE.

WHY SHOULD I TELL *YOU?* YOU'D ONLY *LAUGH,* LIKE THE OTHER NON-BELIEVERS!

BOB, I'D LIKE TO HELP YOU...

NO ONE COULD HELP ME BUT SUPERMAN, AND HE HAS FORSAKEN ME.

I *AM* SUPERMAN, BUT I'M NOT ABOUT TO REVEAL THAT... ESPECIALLY TO SOMEONE WHO THINKS I'M A *GOD!* HOW CAN I GET HIM TO CONFIDE IN CLARK KENT?

DINGALING CIRCUS

3 RINGS 3 UNDER THE BIG TOP

KELLY VOTE

ELECT

SIDEWALK SUPERS

THE BRIEFCASE TRIANGLE

THEATER

ELECT BAR

MAYBE SUPERMAN CAN'T MAKE AN APPEARANCE TO VOUCH FOR ME, BUT A CAREFUL APPLICATION OF HIS *HEAT VISION*--

--WILL MAKE BOB SEE THE LIGHT!

?!?

TRUST KENT

CONTINUED NEXT WEEK!

SUPERMAN ®

Created by
JERRY SIEGEL &
JOE SHUSTER

LAST WEEK: CLARK KENT, SECRETLY SUPERMAN, TRIED TO QUESTION BOB GALT, A YOUNG MAN WHO LITERALLY WORSHIPS SUPERMAN. BUT GALT CONSIDERED KENT A NON-BELIEVER AND REFUSED TO TALK...

TRAINING HIS *HEAT VISION* ON A NEARBY POSTER, KENT GIVES GALT...

A SIGN! MR. KENT...IT'S A SIGN FROM *SUPERMAN!*

TRUST KENT

IT CERTAINLY IS!

WHERE IS HE? HE MUST HAVE BEEN NEARBY, WATCHING OVER US!

"...WHERE WE CAN TALK IN COMPLETE SAFETY!"

THIS HAD BETTER BE *GOOD,* KENT--

--I WAS ALMOST OUT THE DOOR WHEN YOU CALLED. I HAD RINGSIDE SEATS FOR THE FIGHTS!

THIS IS WORTH IT, CHIEF. THREE MEN TRIED TO KILL THIS YOUNG MAN EARLIER TODAY... AND, THOUGH I CAN'T YET PROVE IT, THEY WERE HIRED BY A JUNIOR EXECUTIVE FROM A HIGH-TECH COMPANY OUT ON THE COAST!

EH? WHY?

...I CAN *SHOW* YOU!

WHAT--?!

GREAT CAESAR'S GHOST!!

KENT! WHAT THE DEVIL IS GOING ON? WHERE ARE WE?

DESPITE APPEARANCES, PERRY, I THINK WE'RE STILL IN YOUR OFFICE. THIS... IS SOME SORT OF PRO-JECTION!

THAT'S RIGHT, MR. KENT. IT IS MY POWER TO SHOW OTHERS THINGS I HAVE SEEN ...A POWER I GAINED...

"SHOW & TELL"

ROGER STERN – WRITER
CURT SWAN – PENCILLER
JOHN BEATTY – INKER
BILL OAKLEY – LETTERER
TOM ZIUKO – COLORIST
MIKE CARLIN – EDITOR

NEARER THAN YOU THINK!

IF HE WANTED US TO SEE HIM, BOB, SUPERMAN WOULD HAVE SHOWN HIMSELF BY NOW. BUT DON'T WORRY--

--YOU CAN TELL *ME* ANYTHING YOU WANTED TO TELL SUPERMAN, AND I PROMISE YOU HE'LL HEAR IT. WE'RE... CLOSE.

YES, YOU *MUST* BE. ALL RIGHT, MR. KENT... I WILL.

GREAT! COME ON, I KNOW A PLACE...

THAT'S WHAT I HOPE TO FIND OUT. IT APPARENTLY HAS SOMETHING TO DO WITH BOB'S ...AH... RELIGION. HE WORSHIPS SUPERMAN.

SUPERMAN?!?

OH, LORD! WHY ME?

IT'S OKAY, BOB. MR. WHITE IS ALSO A FRIEND OF SUPERMAN'S ...YOU CAN TALK FREELY HERE. PLEASE...

...TELL US ALL YOU KNOW.

I CAN DO MORE THAN JUST *TELL* YOU, MR. KENT...

...THROUGH LEARNING THE WAY OF THE ONE, TRUE SUPERMAN!

CONTINUED NEXT WEEK!

SUPERMAN® "...BEYOND

Created by
JERRY SIEGEL &
JOE SHUSTER

ANNA MUELLER HAS BEEN CLEANING UP AT THE *DAILY PLANET* FOR YEARS. UNTIL TONIGHT SHE THOUGHT SHE'D HEARD *EVERYTHING!*

IT IS MY POWER TO SHOW OTHERS THINGS I HAVE SEEN... A POWER I GAINED THROUGH LEARNING THE WAY OF THE ONE, TRUE *SUPERMAN!*

?!?

PERRY WHITE
MANAGING EDITOR

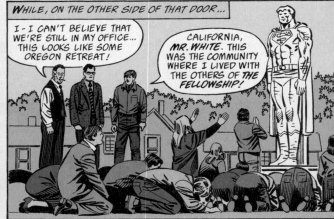

WHILE, ON THE OTHER SIDE OF THAT DOOR...

I - I CAN'T BELIEVE THAT WE'RE STILL IN MY OFFICE... THIS LOOKS LIKE SOME OREGON RETREAT!

CALIFORNIA, *MR. WHITE.* THIS WAS THE COMMUNITY WHERE I LIVED WITH THE OTHERS OF *THE FELLOWSHIP!*

SU-PER-MAN... SU-PER-MAN!

BLAZES! DID YOU HEAR THAT?

SOUND, TOO. THIS ILLUSION HAS EVERYTHING BUT SUBSTANCE.

SU-PER-MAN! SU-PER-MAN!

THIS WAS THE GRAND RITUAL OF THE FELLOWSHIP. THROUGH MEDITATION AND EVOKING HIS NAME, WE, TOO, BEGAN TO GAIN *GREAT POWERS!*

TAKE IT *EASY,* CHIEF! WE'RE NOT REALLY "HERE," REMEMBER? THIS ISN'T REAL.

IT'S REAL ENOUGH FOR *ME,* KENT! YOU HAVEN'T COVERED THE WARS I HAVE!

LORD, THOSE POOR PEOPLE DON'T HAVE A CHANCE!

MORTAL MEN!"

ROGER STERN – SCRIPT
CURT SWAN – PENCILER
JOHN BEATTY – INKER
BILL OAKLEY – LETTERER
TOM ZIUKO – COLORIST
MIKE CARLIN – EDITOR

THIS IS *INCREDIBLE*, KENT... HOW IS YOUNG GALT DOING THIS?

I DON'T KNOW, PERRY. YOU HEARD HIM CLAIM IT CAME FROM WORSHIPING SUPERMAN.

YOU DON'T BELIEVE *THAT?!*

NO...

...BUT MY *X-RAY VISION* DOESN'T SHOW ANY SORT OF PROJECTION DEVICE ON HIM! SOMEHOW, HE'S GENERATED THIS IMAGE ALL AROUND US *HIMSELF!*

BUT IN TIME, THE FELLOWSHIP CAME TO THE ATTENTION OF TOO MANY *NON-BELIEVERS*... TOO LATE WE FOUND OUT THAT WE HAD DEADLY *ENEMIES!*

GOOD LORD!

LOOK OUT! INCOMING!

NO, MR. WHITE... THEY *DIDN'T.* THIS HAPPENED NEARLY A MONTH AGO -- FULLY HALF THE FELLOWSHIP WERE *KILLED.*

THIS IS *MADDENING...*

...PEOPLE ARE DYING ALL AROUND ME AND I CAN'T DO A THING TO SAVE THEM! WHO WAS RESPONSIBLE FOR THIS CARNAGE? *WHO?!*

CONTINUED NEXT WEEK!

LAST ISSUE: BOB GALT TOLD CLARK KENT AND *DAILY PLANET* EDITOR PERRY WHITE OF AN ATTACK ON HIS STRANGE SUPERMAN-WORSHIPPING GROUP-- *THE FELLOWSHIP*-- BY CREATING A 3-D IMAGE OF THE ATTACK!

STOP IT, YOU HEAR? *STOP*--!

CHIEF, NO!

I WOULDN'T MAKE UP SOMETHING THAT HORRIBLE EVEN IF I COULD... MY POWER IS SUCH THAT I CAN SHOW ONLY THAT WHICH I HAVE EXPERIENCED! YOU *STILL* DOUBT ME?

SEE HERE, GALT...YOU CAME IN HERE CLAIMING THAT YOU GAINED POWERS FROM *WORSHIPPING* SUPERMAN! I DON'T CARE IF YOU *DID* TURN MY OFFICE INTO AN OUT-TAKE FROM A GEORGE LUCAS FILM--

--IT STILL SEEMS PRETTY FAR-FETCHED TO ME! IF THAT ATTACK DID HAPPEN, WHY DIDN'T YOU CALL IN THE POLICE... OR THE F.B.I.?

YOU SAID THAT HALF OF THE FELLOWSHIP WERE KILLED... WHAT HAPPENED TO THE *SURVIVORS*?

AT THAT MOMENT, SOME THREE THOUSAND MILES AWAY...

GENTLEMEN, I HAVE BAD NEWS--

--TODAY, ONE OF OUR AGENTS FAILED TO TERMINATE A FELLOWSHIP COURIER. INFORMATION IS SKETCHY... WE'RE NOT CERTAIN, BUT THE COURIER MAY HAVE MADE CONTACT WITH *SUPERMAN*!

NO! IF SUPERMAN EVEN *SUSPECTS* OUR EXISTENCE--!

LURKS THE EVIL?"

ROGER STERN – WRITER
CURT SWAN – PENCILLER
JOHN BEATTY – INKER
BILL OAKLEY – LETTERER
TOM ZIUKO – COLORIST
MIKE CARLIN – EDITOR

THEY'RE JUST *IMAGES*, PERRY... THERE'S NOTHING WE CAN DO. NOT EVEN SUPERMAN COULD SAVE THEM.

YOU'VE MADE YOUR POINT, GALT... YOU CAN STOP THE PICTURE SHOW!

GLADLY, MR. KENT. I ONLY WISH--

-- I COULD AS EASILY BANISH THE IMAGES FROM MY *MIND!*

INCREDIBLE! AND EVERYTHING YOU SHOWED US, GALT... THOSE FELLOWSHIP PEOPLE, THE ATTACK... ALL THAT REALLY HAPPENED?

THOSE OF US WHO SURVIVED WENT INTO HIDING. WE WERE AFRAID TO CONTACT THE AUTHORITIES... FOR FEAR OF BEING TRACKED DOWN BY OUR ATTACKERS.

I WAS CHOSEN TO SEEK OUT THE ONE MAN WE KNEW WE COULD TRUST... *SUPERMAN*... AND ASK FOR HIS HELP!

KENT, I DON'T KNOW *WHAT* TO BELIEVE! IF YOU WANT THIS STORY, IT'S YOUR BABY. BUT YOU'D BETTER FIND ME SOME HARD EVIDENCE.

KENT?

SORRY, CHIEF. I WAS JUST WONDERING... WHO WOULD COMMIT SO MUCH MONEY AND EFFORT TO KILLING THOSE PEOPLE... AND *WHY?*

WE MUST ASSUME THE WORST...

... WE MUST BE PREPARED TO *DESTROY* HIM! IT'S THE ONLY WAY *THIS WORLD* CAN BE *SAVED!*

CONTINUED NEXT WEEK!

SUPERMAN "WICKED

Created by
JERRY SIEGEL &
JOE SHUSTER

SUPERMAN REMAINS THE GREATEST CHALLENGE TO OUR WAY OF LIFE... OUR CONSORTIUM CANNOT REST UNTIL HE IS NO MORE!

HE'S A HERO TO THE MASSES... WE SHOULD PUBLICLY DISCREDIT HIM FIRST!

THAT WOULD TAKE TOO LONG. NO, GENTLEMEN, WE MUST ELIMINATE HIM!

HODGES, YOU IMPLIED THAT A FELLOWSHIP COURIER MAY HAVE WARNED SUPERMAN ABOUT US... HOW COULD SUCH A THING HAPPEN?

ONE OF OUR AGENTS WAS ASSIGNED TO PREVENT ANY CONTACT BETWEEN THE FELLOWSHIP AND SUPERMAN-- BUT HE BOTCHED THE JOB. HE ACTUALLY LET SUPERMAN CAPTURE HIM!

MY ASSISTANT GOT THE FULL STORY FROM AGENT CULPEPPER AS THEY RUSHED HIM TO THE HOSPITAL. IT IS REGRETABLE, BUT WE MUST NOW MAKE CERTAIN THAT HE NEVER REPEATS THAT STORY.

MEANWHILE, ON THE OTHER SIDE OF THE NATION...

IT'S REALLY GOOD OF YOU TO PUT ME UP AT YOUR PLACE, MR. KENT! THIS IS REALLY SOMETHING!

I DOUBT ANYONE ELSE WILL COME GUNNING FOR YOUNG MR. GALT IN MY APARTMENT. AND WITH HIM SAFELY TUCKED AWAY--

--I'M FREE TO TRACK DOWN WHOEVER IT IS WHO WANTS TO WIPE OUT HIM AND HIS BIZARRE SUPERMAN-WORSHIPPING FELLOWSHIP.

I'D SWEAR THE MAN BEHIND THIS AFTERNOON'S ATTEMPT ON BOB'S LIFE IS THE SAME MAN THE WIRE SERVICES PLACED IN A CALIFORNIA BURN CENTER.

BUSINESS!"

ROGER STERN – WRITER
CURT SWAN – PENCILLER
MURPHY ANDERSON – INKER
BILL OAKLEY – LETTERER
PETRA SCOTESE – COLORIST
MIKE CARLIN – EDITOR

"LUCKILY, HE WAS EQUIPPED WITH OUR EXPERIMENTAL **MASS TELEPORTER.** IT TRANSPORTED HIM AWAY FROM SUPERMAN... AND TO MY FIRM'S BAKERSFIELD LABS... SOMEWHAT THE WORSE FOR THE EXPERIENCE."

CONSIDERING MY RENT, IT'D BETTER BE! HELP YOURSELF TO THE REFRIGERATOR, **BOB,** IF YOU FEEL HUNGRY.

I HAVE A FEW... ERRANDS TO RUN. LET'S LOCK THIS DOOR, OKAY? AND IF ANYONE KNOCKS, DON'T ANSWER. I CAN LET MYSELF IN.

WHATEVER YOU SAY, SIR.

MAYBE I CAN GET SOME ANSWERS OUT OF THIS CHARLES CULPEPPER...

"...ASSUMING HE'S IN ANY CONDITION TO TALK."

'EVENING, MR. CULPEPPER. TIME TO... CHECK OUT!

CONTINUED NEXT WEEK!

I CAN ALMOST ACCEPT THAT THIS SECRET *FELLOWSHIP* CONSIDERS ME A *GOD*... AFTER ALL, THERE ARE A LOT OF STRANGE CULTS IN CALIFORNIA.

BUT IF BOB GALT IS TO BE BELIEVED, THEY ARE ALSO GAINING BIZARRE *POWERS*... THROUGH WORSHIPPING ME! *THAT* I CANNOT ACCEPT!

A MAN WHO'S A PERFECT MATCH FOR BOB'S WOULD-BE KILLER WAS ADMITTED TO THIS *BURN CENTER* SHORTLY AFTER THE EXPLOSION.

IF IT *IS* THE SAME MAN, HOW DID HE GET SOME *3,000 MILES* FROM METROPOLIS IN A MATTER OF MINUTES?! SO MANY QUESTIONS...

...IT'S TIME I STARTED GETTING SOME *ANSWERS!*

EXCUSE ME, I UNDERSTAND YOU'RE TREATING A *CHARLES CULPEPPER* HERE... WOULD IT BE POSSIBLE FOR ME TO SPEAK WITH HIM?

S-SUPERMAN! YES... *NO!* I MEAN... *MR.* CULPEPPER IS HERE... BUT HE'S RESTING NOW AND SHOULDN'T HAVE VISITORS!

BUT AS THE MAN OF STEEL FOCUSES HIS AMAZING X-RAY VISION...

GOOD LORD!

SUPERMAN, WHAT--?!

TELL YOUR SECURITY TO MEET ME AT CULPEPPER'S ROOM! AND *HURRY--*

COMES CALLING...

ROGER STERN – WRITER
CURT SWAN – PENCILLER
MURPHY ANDERSON – INKER
BILL OAKLEY – LETTERER
TOM ZIUKO – COLORIST
MIKE CARLIN – EDITOR

THERE MUST BE SOMETHING ELSE THAT'S BEHIND THEIR POWERS... QUESTION IS, *WHAT?* I CAN'T IGNORE THAT BOB CAME ALL THE WAY TO METROPOLIS TO ENLIST MY HELP FOR THE FELLOWSHIP--

--AND A MAN TRIED TO *KILL* HIM FOR HIS EFFORTS! THAT MAN ESCAPED ME BY *BLOWING HIMSELF UP...* OR SO IT *SEEMED!*

CAN YOU AT LEAST TELL ME HIS ROOM NUMBER?

Y-YES, OF COURSE. HE'S IN ROOM 256.

THAT'S IN THE NORTH WING? YES... I SEE...

"--THE MAN'S LIFE IS IN DANGER!"

SORRY 'BOUT THIS, CULPEPPER! NOTHING PERSONAL, YOU UNDERSTAND!

GET AWAY FROM THAT MAN-- *NOW!!*

KER-RAK!

CONTINUED NEXT WEEK!

SUPERMAN ®

Created by
JERRY SIEGEL &
JOE SHUSTER

FATAL

Arriving at a California burn center to question a man about an attempted murder, the man of steel finds that his suspect is about to become another victim...

SUPERMAN?! **HERE**?!?

DIDN'T YOU **HEAR** ME? I SAID--

--GET AWAY--

WHAT'S GOING ON IN--? **HOLEE**--!!

LOOKS LIKE YOU GOT HERE JUST IN TIME TO SAVE HIS LIFE, SUPERMAN... THOUGH WHAT **KIND** OF LIFE HE'LL HAVE, I CAN'T SAY.

HE'S **COMATOSE**... ONLY TIME WILL TELL IF THERE'S BRAIN DAMAGE.

UH... SUPERMAN? Y-YOU MUST'VE HIT THIS OTHER GUY **TOO HARD**...

FLAW?

ROGER STERN – WRITER
CURT SWAN – PENCILLER
MURPHY ANDERSON – INKER
BILL OAKLEY – LETTERER
TOM ZIUKO – COLORIST
MIKE CARLIN – EDITOR

--FROM THAT MAN...

...NOW!

WHAM!

YOU SAY HE WAS SUFFOCATING--?

HE WAS *BEING SUFFOCATED* BY A MAN DRESSED AS AN ORDERLY... THOUGH I'D BE SURPRISED IF THE MAN ACTUALLY WORKS HERE!

...HE'S *DEAD!*

CONTINUED NEXT WEEK!

MOVING QUICKLY TO PREVENT A MURDER, SUPERMAN SENT THE ASSASSIN SLAMMING INTO A WALL...

NO PULSE, NO RESPIRATION... HE'S DEAD, ALL RIGHT!

BUT *HOW!*

YOU HAD TO ACT FAST TO STOP HIM FROM KILLING THAT POOR FELLOW, SUPERMAN. IF YOU HIT HIM A LITTLE TOO HARD... WELL, NOBODY'S GONNA BLAME YOU--!

NONSENSE! I DIDN'T HIT HIM HARD ENOUGH TO DO ANY MORE THAN KNOCK THE WIND OUT OF HIM!

SOON...

YOU WERE RIGHT, SUPERMAN. IT APPEARS THAT SOME KIND OF *TRANSCEIVER* HAS BEEN SURGICALLY IMPLANTED IN THE MASTOID SINUS.

HMM, YES... THE MICRO-MINIATURIZATION IS *ASTOUNDING!* NEVER SEEN ANYTHING LIKE IT!

SUCH A TRANSCEIVER WOULD PICK UP ANYTHING THIS MAN HEARD AND TRANSMIT IT TO WHOMEVER WAS MONITORING ITS FREQUENCY. IT COULD ALSO RECEIVE INCOMING SIGNALS.

FRABOOM

TELL NO TALES"

ROGER STERN - WRITER
CURT SWAN - PENCILLER
MURPHY ANDERSON - INKER
BILL OAKLEY - LETTERER
PETRA SCOTESE - COLORIST
MIKE CARLIN - EDITOR

THEN WHAT KILLED HIM?

GOOD QUESTION. LET'S HAVE A LOOK...

GAZING BENEATH THE SURFACE OF THE MAN'S BODY WITH HIS UNCANNY X-RAY VISION...

AH-HAH! THERE'S SOMETHING THAT'S NOT FACTORY EQUIPMENT! FIVE WILL GET YOU TEN THAT HOLDS THE ANSWER!

AND WHOEVER WAS LISTENING IN SOMEHOW USED THE IMPLANT TO KILL HIM, CORRECT?

A REASONABLE ASSUMPTION! HE CERTAINLY WASN'T KILLED BY YOUR BLOW. OF COURSE, WE'LL KNOW MORE AFTER AN AUTOPSY.

WAIT A MINUTE! THAT TRANSCEIVER IS STILL FUNCTIONING!

WHAT?

LATER... ...PROBABLY SOME KIND OF PLASTIC EXPLOSIVE. IT'LL BE HARD TO TELL, THOUGH... THERE'S NOT MUCH LEFT TO EXAMINE.

ARE YOU TWO SURE YOU'RE ALL RIGHT?

I- I GUESS SO, SUPERMAN. IT'S JUST... DEALING WITH ACCIDENT VICTIMS, I'VE SEEN SOME PRETTY AWFUL STUFF, BUT THAT--! WHO WOULD DO SUCH A THING?

I DON'T KNOW, DOCTOR... BUT I INTEND TO FIND OUT!

CONTINUED NEXT WEEK!

SUPERMAN
Created by
JERRY SIEGEL &
JOE SHUSTER

LAST ISSUE: SUPERMAN DISCOVERED THAT THE WOULD-BE ASSASSIN OF CHARLES CULPEPPER HAD BEEN KILLED BY REMOTE CONTROL -- THROUGH A RADIO TRANSCEIVER IMPLANTED IN HIS SKULL.

AFTER GIVING A STATEMENT TO THE LOCAL AUTHORITIES...

TO THINK THAT THE KILLER WAS WALKING AROUND WITH A MINIATURE *BOMB* IN HIS HEAD! WHY WOULD HE LET THAT BE DONE TO HIM?

YEAH, AND WHY DID THIS GUY TRY TO KILL CULPEPPER ANYWAY?

GOOD QUESTIONS... ONCE WE ANSWER ONE, WE'LL PROBABLY HAVE THE ANSWER TO THE OTHER.

I SUSPECT THAT THE ATTEMPT WAS MADE ON CULPEPPER'S LIFE TO KEEP HIM FROM ANSWERING MY QUESTIONS. IF I'D GOTTEN TO HIM A LITTLE SOONER, MAYBE HE WOULDN'T BE IN A *COMA* NOW!

I CAN'T PROVE IT, BUT--

-- I'M SURE CULPEPPER WAS PART OF A PLOT TO EXTERMINATE THAT *FELLOWSHIP* OF MISGUIDED SOULS WHO WORSHIP ME AS IF I WERE A GOD!

-- I HOPE HE'S GETTING ALONG ALL RIGHT.

BRINGING HIS ASTOUNDING *X-RAY* AND *TELESCOPIC* VISIONS INTO PLAY, THE MAN OF STEEL FOCUSES ON THE GREAT METROPOLIS, STILL MILES AWAY.

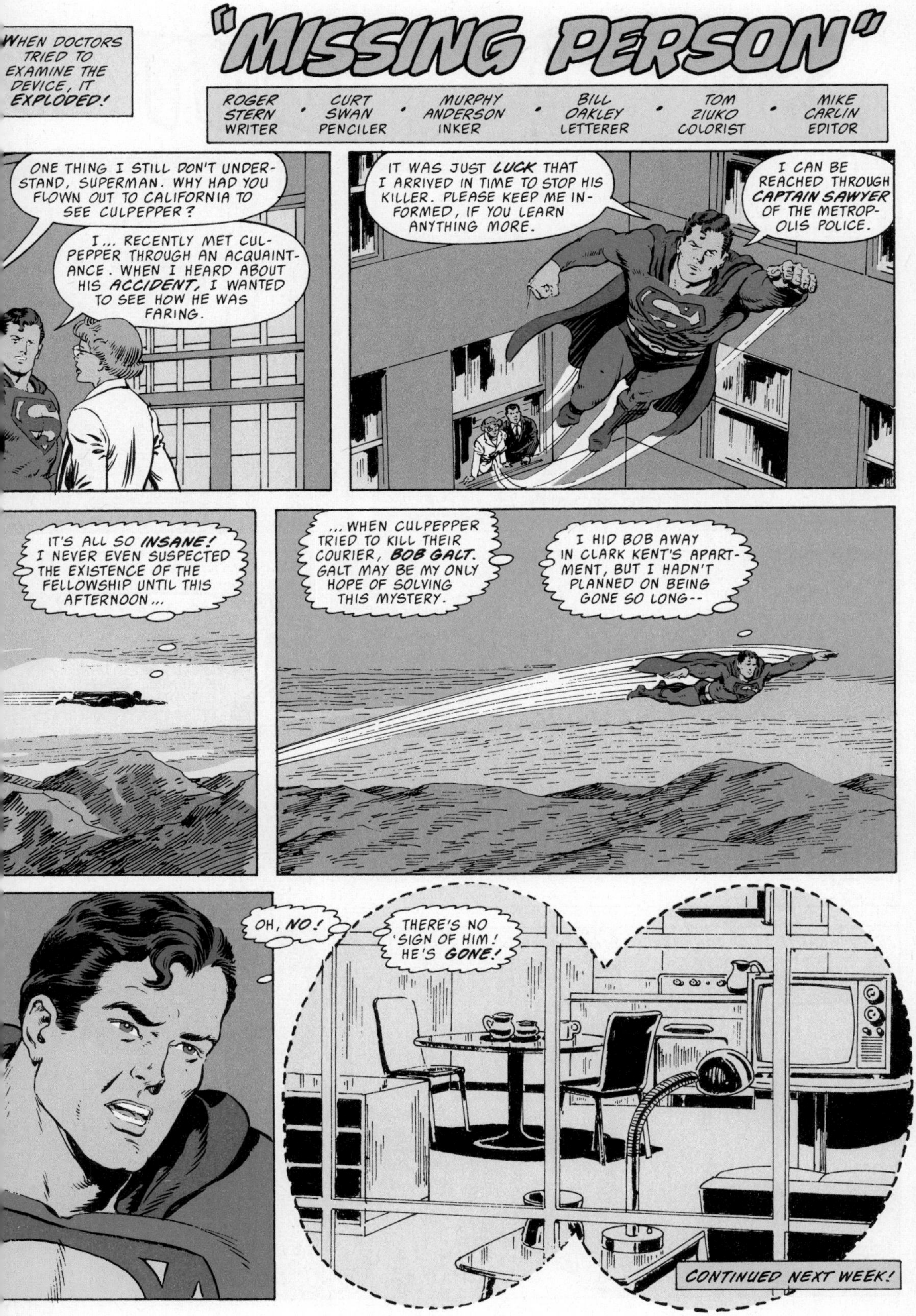

WHEN DOCTORS TRIED TO EXAMINE THE DEVICE, IT EXPLODED!
"MISSING PERSON"
ROGER STERN WRITER • CURT SWAN PENCILER • MURPHY ANDERSON INKER • BILL OAKLEY LETTERER • TOM ZIUKO COLORIST • MIKE CARLIN EDITOR
ONE THING I STILL DON'T UNDERSTAND, SUPERMAN. WHY HAD YOU FLOWN OUT TO CALIFORNIA TO SEE CULPEPPER?
I... RECENTLY MET CULPEPPER THROUGH AN ACQUAINTANCE. WHEN I HEARD ABOUT HIS ACCIDENT, I WANTED TO SEE HOW HE WAS FARING.
IT WAS JUST LUCK THAT I ARRIVED IN TIME TO STOP HIS KILLER. PLEASE KEEP ME INFORMED, IF YOU LEARN ANYTHING MORE.
I CAN BE REACHED THROUGH CAPTAIN SAWYER OF THE METROPOLIS POLICE.
IT'S ALL SO INSANE! I NEVER EVEN SUSPECTED THE EXISTENCE OF THE FELLOWSHIP UNTIL THIS AFTERNOON...
...WHEN CULPEPPER TRIED TO KILL THEIR COURIER, BOB GALT. GALT MAY BE MY ONLY HOPE OF SOLVING THIS MYSTERY.
I HID BOB AWAY IN CLARK KENT'S APARTMENT, BUT I HADN'T PLANNED ON BEING GONE SO LONG--
OH, NO!
THERE'S NO SIGN OF HIM! HE'S GONE!
CONTINUED NEXT WEEK!

SUPERMAN®

"OUT ON

RETURNING TO THE CLINTON STREET APARTMENT HE MAINTAINS AS CLARK KENT, SUPERMAN DISCOVERS THAT HIS GUEST BOB GALT IS...

MISSING! NOT A TRACE OF HIM!

WHAT?!?

Mr. Kent—
Got tired of sitting around. Going out to see the sights. Don't worry... Superman will protect me!

Bob

MOMENTS LATER...

SURE, MR. KENT... I SAW HIM. HE MUST'VE LEFT HERE ABOUT 15... 20 MINUTES AGO. I'M NOT SURE, BUT I THINK HE HEADED DOWNTOWN.

"...OR WHAT SORT OF TROUBLE HE'S GETTING INTO!"

SACRILEGE!

½ OFF SALE

I ♥ METRO

WHAT'RE YOU... ON DRUGS OR JUST PLAIN CRAZY?!

T-SHIRTS ALL SIZES ½ OFF

SPORT YOUR TENNIS ALL SIZ

THE TOWN"

ROGER STERN – WRITER
CURT SWAN – PENCILLER
MURPHY ANDERSON – INKER
BILL OAKLEY – LETTERER
TOM ZIUKO – COLORIST
MIKE CARLIN – EDITOR

NO SIGNS OF FOUL PLAY... BUT THE ENEMIES OF BOB'S FELLOWSHIP GROUP ARE AS INGENIOUS AS THEY ARE RUTHLESS. IF THEY MANAGED TO TRACE HIM HERE, THEY MIGHT HAVE LURED HIM AWAY ON SOME RUSE.

WAIT A MINUTE... WHAT'S *THIS?*

WONDERFUL! IN A CITY AS BIG AS METROPOLIS, ANYTHING COULD HAPPEN IN 15 MINUTES! THERE'S NO TELLING WHERE BOB'S GONE!

SUPERMAN IS OUR INSPIRATION ...OUR SAVIOUR! TO EXPLOIT HIS SYMBOL IN THIS WAY IS THE WORST BLASPHEMY! IT WILL NOT GO UNPUNISHED!

N-NEITHER WILL THAT DAMAGE! LISTEN... I-I'M WARNIN' YOU, MAN, ONE STEP CLOSER--

--AN' YOU'RE *HISTORY!*

CONTINUED NEXT WEEK!

SUPERMAN® "PROTECTIVE"

Created by
JERRY SIEGEL &
JOE SHUSTER

SOMEWHERE DOWN THERE AMONG ELEVEN MILLION PEOPLE IS ONE MISGUIDED YOUNG MAN WHO LOOKS ON ME AS HIS *GOD AND PROTECTOR!*

I MUST FIND HIM! WITH THAT KIND OF ATTITUDE...

"...HE'S *BOUND* TO GET INTO TROUBLE!"

I WILL NOT TOLERATE THIS EXPLOITATION OF SUPERMAN'S HOLY SYMBOL!

SHORTLY...

...HE TOOK ONE LOOK AT THE SUPERMAN SHIRTS AND WENT *WILD!* I WAS JUST DEFENDING MYSELF! I THOUGHT HE WAS ON DRUGS...

WHAT KIND OF MAN MAKES MONEY BY EXPLOITING THE SACRED 'S'?

AWRIGHT, THAT'S *ENOUGH!*

LOOK, FELLA, THIS MAN ISN'T BREAKING ANY LAWS. BESIDES, SUPERMAN HIMSELF *APPROVED* THE MARKETING OF THOSE SHIRTS... THE PROCEEDS GO TO THE *METROPOLIS UNITED CHARITIES.*

I SHALL NOT MAKE SUCH AN ERROR AGAIN! MAY SUPERMAN BLESS YOU!

I THOUGHT I'D SEEN ALL KINDS, BUT... A SUPER-MAN WORSHIPER?

PROBABLY FROM CALIFORNIA.

SHIELD?"

ROGER STERN - WRITER
CURT SWAN - PENCILLER
MURPHY ANDERSON - INKER
BILL OAKLEY - LETTERER
TOM ZIUKO - COLORIST
MIKE CARLIN - EDITOR

HOLY--? L-LOOK, I KNOW HOW TO USE THIS THING! YOU TAKE ONE MORE STEP, AN' SO HELP ME--!

HOLD IT-- BOTH OF YOU!

GIVE ME THAT GUN AND WE'LL TALK THIS OVER, OKAY?

CHARITY? I-I DIDN'T KNOW.

I ACTED UNTHINKINGLY... OUT OF IGNORANCE. PLEASE ALLOW ME TO MAKE *AMENDS* FOR THE DAMAGE I HAVE DONE. IT IS WHAT SUPER-MAN WOULD WANT!

WELL... AH... ALL RIGHT.

I SHOULD HAVE KNOWN THAT SUPERMAN WOULD ALLOW THE DISTRIBUTION OF SUCH *ICONS* IN THE CITY WHERE HE IS BEST KNOWN.

I FEEL DOUBLY BLESSED TO BE WEARING HIS SACRED SYM-BOL. SURELY NO HARM WILL BEFALL ME *NOW!*

CONTINUED NEXT WEEK!

Created by
JERRY SIEGEL &
JOE SHUSTER

WHAT HAVE WE *HERE?* LOOKS LIKE A TOURIST!

NICE SHOES. MAYBE I'LL TAKE THOSE NICE SHOES, HUH?

YEAH, BUT YOU CAN KEEP THAT SHIRT! I DON'T WANNA LOOK LIKE *SUPER-WASTE!*

INFIDELS! HOW *DARE* YOU MOCK THE BLESSED SUPERMAN? YOU AREN'T FIT TO TOUCH HIS CAPE!

≥HAUK~

PTUU!

SMEK

SUPER-BOY HERE IS ALL MINE!

WHEE-HEE-HEE! GIT 'IM, SKUD!

CAREFUL O' HIS SHOES! HAW!

THE HERO?"

ROGER STERN – WRITER
CURT SWAN – PENCILLER
MURPHY ANDERSON – INKER
BILL OAKLEY – LETTERER
TOM ZIUKO – COLORIST
MIKE CARLIN – EDITOR

OOO! HE'S RIGHT! HOW *DARE* WE?

I CAN'T LIVE WIT' MYSELF! I'LL NEVER TOUCH HIS CAPE!

LAUGH ALL YOU WANT! SUPERMAN IS MY *PROTECTOR!*

HEY!

'SOKAY! I DON'T NEED NO HELP!

SO WHERE'S YER BIG-DEAL "PROTECTOR", KID? HUH? WHERE IS HE?

HA-HAH-HA!

CONTINUED NEXT WEEK!

45

SUPERMAN®

Created by
JERRY SIEGEL &
JOE SHUSTER

AFTER A FRANTIC SEARCH, *SUPERMAN* HAS FINALLY FOUND *BOB GALT* IN A DOWNTOWN METROPOLIS ALLEY...

IF YOU'VE DONE THAT YOUNG MAN ANY *PERMANENT* HARM, I *SWEAR* YOU'LL LIVE TO REGRET IT!

%#@!!! RUN FOR IT!

HOW? THE ONLY WAY OUTTA HERE IS *THROUGH HIM!*

ZIPPO, *HELP!* DO SOMETHING!

DON'T WORRY... YOU'LL BE TOGETHER WITH YOUR FRIENDS IN NO TIME AT ALL!

MOMENTS LATER...

OWW... WHAT--?

TAKE IT EASY, BOB. YOU'RE GOING TO BE *SORE* FOR A FEW DAYS, BUT I THINK YOU'LL BE ALL RIGHT.

PUNISHMENT CRIME"

ROGER STERN - WRITER
CURT SWAN - PENCILLER
MURPHY ANDERSON - INKER
BILL OAKLEY - LETTERER
TOM ZIUKO - COLORIST
MIKE CARLIN - EDITOR

IF THAT'S THE WAY IT'S GOTTA BE--! I HEARD THAT BULLETS CAN'T HURT YA, BIG MAN... BUT HOW ARE YA WITH *KNIVES?*

AKTINK

UH-OH.

BONK

WHUD

KTANG

YOU...YOU *SAVED* ME, DIDN'T YOU? JUST LIKE I KNEW YOU WOULD...

...MR. KENT?

CONTINUED NEXT WEEK!

SUPERMAN®

Created by JERRY SIEGEL & JOE SHUSTER

"SEEDS

IT'S A GOOD THING I FOUND YOU WHEN I DID, BOB... LOOKS LIKE YOU TOOK QUITE A *BEATING!*

I DON'T UNDERSTAND, *MR. KENT...* I THOUGHT *SUPERMAN* WOULD PROTECT ME...

BOB, I KNOW THAT YOU AND YOUR FRIENDS *WORSHIP* SUPERMAN, BUT YOU HAVE TO FACE FACTS!

SUPERMAN CAN'T BE *EVERYWHERE!* FOR ALL HIS POWERS, HE ISN'T ALL-SEEING OR ALL-KNOWING...

I THINK I SHOULD MEET THESE *ELDERS,* BOB. WILL YOU TAKE ME TO THEM?

OF COURSE, MR. KENT. BUT... I'M STILL CONFUSED ...WHAT HAPPENED TO THE HOODLUMS WHO ATTACKED ME HERE?

...BUT OUR *CONSORTIUM* FACES A GRAVE CRISIS. LAST NIGHT, SUPERMAN STOPPED ONE OF OUR SPECIAL AGENTS FROM TERMINATING CHARLES CULPEPPER!

WHAT?!? IF CULPEPPER TALKS--!

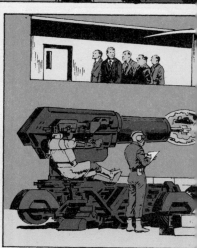

# of DOUBT"

ROGER STERN – WRITER
CURT SWAN – PENCILER
MURPHY ANDERSON – INKER
BILL OAKLEY – LETTERER
TOM ZIUKO – COLORIST
MIKE CARLIN – EDITOR

...IF HE WAS, HE WOULD'VE SAVED YOUR *FELLOWSHIP* GROUP FROM ITS ENEMIES... WOULDN'T HE?

I-I GUESS YOU'RE RIGHT. BUT THE GROUP ELDERS TAUGHT US THAT SUPERMAN WAS OUR *SAVIOUR*.

I... AH... CAN'T SAY, BOB. PERHAPS SOMETHING SCARED THEM OFF.

¿UHHGH?

MEANWHILE, THREE THOUSAND MILES TO THE WEST...

I APOLOGIZE FOR CALLING YOU HERE ON SUCH SHORT NOTICE, GENTLEMEN...

SEQUOIA TECHTRONICS
EXPERIMENTAL RESEARCH FACILITY

HE WON'T... AT LEAST FOR NOW. HE'S IN A COMA. AND THE *ASSASSIN* WE SENT HAS PAID THE PRICE FOR HIS FAILURE.

BUT DON'T YOU *SEE?* SUPERMAN MUST HAVE CONNECTED CULPEPPER TO OUR OPERATION TO ELIMINATE THE FELLOWSHIP ...HE MAY ALREADY KNOW THAT CULPEPPER WORKED FOR MY COMPANY!

GENTLEMEN, OUR *WORST FEARS* HAVE BEEN REALIZED! WE MUST DIVERT ALL OUR RESOURCES TO THE GOALS OF THE CONSORTIUM.

WE MUST *DESTROY SUPERMAN*, BEFORE HE DESTROYS *US!*

NEXT WEEK:
THE REASON WHY!

HERE, GENTLEMEN, IS EVIDENCE OF HOW FAR THE CONSORTIUM HAS COME IN JUST A YEAR. TOGETHER, POOLING OUR SEPARATE COMPANIES' RE-SOURCES IN SECRET--

--WE'VE MADE BREAKTHROUGHS IN MICRO-ELECTRONICS AND SOLID-STATE PHYSICS... DECADES AHEAD OF THEIR TIME!

THOSE BREAKTHROUGHS WOULD MAKE US THE DOMINANT FORCE IN THE WORLD ECONOMY, HODGES. WHEN WILL WE BE ALLOWED TO MAKE *COMMERCIAL USE* OF THEM?

YOU CAN SEE HOW THE TEEMING MASSES WOULD-- IN THEIR *IGNO-RANCE*-- LOOK UP TO HIM.

THERE HAVE BEEN OTHER COSTUMED HEROES, BUT NEVER ANYONE REMOTELY LIKE HIM. HIS FEATS BECAME THE STUFF OF *LEGEND*...

... AND WITH HIS POWERS AND ABILITIES, SUPERMAN CAPTURED THE PUBLIC'S IMAGINATION IMMEDIATELY.

I REMEMBER THINKING HE WAS TOO GOOD TO BE TRUE. IN TIME, WE LEARNED THAT INDEED WAS THE CASE...

THE *FOOLS!* THE EVIDENCE WAS RIGHT BEFORE THEIR EYES... BUT THEY CHOSE TO IGNORE IT.

PEOPLE'S ADMIRATION TURNED TO HERO-WORSHIP... AND IN THE CASE OF THE DAMNED *FELLOWSHIP,* TO OUTRIGHT WORSHIP.

WHEN I LEARNED THAT THE FELLOWSHIP CULTISTS WERE WORSHIPING *GRAVEN IMAGES* OF SUPERMAN -- AND THAT SOME OF THEM WERE ACTUALLY GAINING *POWERS* -- I KNEW THAT THE SO-CALLED MAN OF STEEL...

LATIONS"

ROGER STERN – WRITER
CURT SWAN – PENCILLER
MURPHY ANDERSON – INKER
BILL OAKLEY – LETTERER
TOM ZIUKO – COLORIST
MIKE CARLIN – EDITOR

PATIENCE, BILLINGS! BEFORE WE CAN BRING ABOUT A NEW GOLDEN AGE FOR MANKIND, WE MUST FIRST ELIMINATE THE *GREAT BEAST* OF THE *APOCALYPSE*...

...THE MONSTER WHO CALLS ITSELF *SUPERMAN!*

DAILY PLANET

SUPERMAN: ALIEN VISITOR, SOLE SURVIVOR OF DEAD PLANET.

...BUT EVEN THAT REVELATION DIDN'T COOL THE PUBLIC'S ADORATION FOR THIS... THIS *INHUMAN CREATURE!*

...COULD ONLY BE THE LONG-PROPHESIED *ANTICHRIST!*

WE OWE YOU AN INCALCULABLE DEBT FOR WARNING US OF SUPERMAN'S TRUE NATURE, HODGES.

IT WAS MY *SACRED DUTY* TO BRING MY DISCOVERY TO LIKE-MINDED MEN. ONLY BY WORKING TOGETHER COULD WE SAVE HUMANITY FROM THIS *HIDDEN EVIL.*

AND NOW, WITH OUR TECHNOLOGICAL MIGHT, WE ACTUALLY HAVE A CHANCE OF WIPING SUPERMAN AND HIS UNHOLY WORSHIPERS *FROM THE FACE OF THE EARTH!!*

CONTINUED NEXT WEEK!

Created by
JERRY SIEGEL &
JOE SHUSTER

"PIN

ROBERT GALT IS THE MESSENGER WHO EVADED US IN METROPOLIS, GENTLEMEN... WE MUST FIND HIM!

HE IS THE KEY TO THE EXTERMINATION NOT ONLY OF HIS CURSED *FELLOWSHIP*-- BUT OF *SUPERMAN*, AS WELL!

MEANWHILE, BACK IN METROPOLIS...

SOON...

DEPARTURES LEVEL B

BUT, MR. KENT--

--SHOULDN'T WE HAVE STOPPED AT THE TICKET COUNTER?

NO NEED, BOB. I'VE ALREADY ARRANGED OUR FLIGHT.

NO ADMITTANCE

BUT THIS ISN'T A PASSENGER PLANE!

IT IS FOR *US*! I KNOW THE PILOT!

THE TAIL..."

ROGER STERN – WRITER
CURT SWAN – PENCILLER
MURPHY ANDERSON – INKER
BILL OAKLEY – LETTERER
TOM ZIUKO – COLORIST
MIKE CARLIN – EDITOR

IF I CAN MEET THE REST OF THESE SUPERMAN-WORSHIPING *CULTISTS*, MAYBE I'LL BE ABLE TO DISCOVER WHO'S TRYING TO *KILL* THEM... AND WHY THEIR ENEMIES HATE ME SO MUCH!

COME ON, BOB, LET'S GO!

HUH? WHERE, MR. KENT?

CALIFORNIA! YOU PROMISED TO TAKE ME TO THE ELDERS OF YOUR FELLOWSHIP, REMEMBER?

HMM... I SEE THAT WE'VE PICKED UP A *TAIL*. THE FELLOWSHIP'S ENEMIES PROBABLY HAVE ALL THE MAJOR TRANSPORTATION CENTERS STAKED OUT. THIS ENEMY'S AGENTS HAVE A BAD HABIT OF *EXPLODING...*

...CAN'T RISK A CONFRONTATION IN A CROWDED AIRPORT!

COME ON, BOB-- *THIS* WAY!

HEY! WHERE DO *YOU* THINK YOU'RE GOING?

I...SAW AN OLD FRIEND... I WAS GOIN' TO SAY HELLO!

NO ADMITTANCE

NOT THROUGH *THERE*, YOU'RE NOT!

GOOD TO SEE YOU AGAIN, CLARK!

YOU GUYS BETTER STRAP YOURSELVES IN! AS SOON AS I GET CLEARANCE FROM THE TOWER--

"--WE ARE OUTTA HERE!"

HE WON'T LOSE US THIS EASILY!

GALT AND ANOTHER MAN JUST TOOK OFF ON A COURIER PLANE... DESTINATION UNKNOWN. PASS THE WORD TO OUR OPERATIVES IN THE COURIER INDUSTRY ...FULL ALERT!

NEXT WEEK: CALIFORNIA BOUND!

SUPERMAN®

Created by
JERRY SIEGEL &
JOE SHUSTER

LAST WEEK: EN ROUTE TO CALIFORNIA TO FIND THE *ELDERS OF THE FELLOWSHIP*, CLARK KENT AND BOB GALT EVADED AGENTS OF THE MYSTERIOUS *CONSORTIUM* BY BOARDING A COURIER PLANE...

"OUT

...SO YOU SEE, *MR. KENT*, ONLY BY LETTING SUPERMAN INTO OUR HEARTS CAN WE TRULY KNOW *TRUTH* AND *JUSTICE*!

¿SIGH? I THOUGHT I WAS BEGINNING TO CONVINCE YOU THAT *SUPERMAN* ISN'T A *GOD*, BOB.

YOUR ARGUMENTS HAVE *TESTED* ME, MR. KENT-- BUT THE *FAITH* OF THE FELLOWSHIP IS STRONG ENOUGH TO *BEND STEEL*!

MM-HMMM.

HE HASN'T LET UP SINCE WE LEFT METROPOLIS!

THE PLANE CARRYING GALT SHOULD LAND SOMEWHERE IN THIS STATE! I WANT ALL PERSONNEL-- RIGHT DOWN TO OUR *CLEANING CREWS*-- TO WATCH FOR HIM AND REPORT *DIRECTLY* TO THIS COMMAND POST!

IT WILL BE DONE, HODGES!

BARELY AN HOUR LATER, THE CONSORTIUM'S TARGET DEPLANES AT A SOUTHERN CALIFORNIA AIRPORT...

...HE AND KENT BEGIN THE FINAL LEG OF THEIR JOURNEY!

U·RENT·IT
-A SEQUOIA TECKTRONICS COMPANY-
EXIT · DO NOT ENTER · EXIT

STILL NO SIGNS OF ANYONE ON OUR TAIL! I CAN'T BELIEVE THINGS ARE GOING SO *SMOOTHLY*!

DID YOU PLANT THE DEVICE?

ROGER STERN / WRITER
CURT SWAN / PENCILLER
MURPHY ANDERSON / INKER
BILL OAKLEY / LETTERER
TOM ZIUKO / COLORIST
MIKE CARLIN / EDITOR

THIS IS THE LAST TIME I FLY 3,000 MILES WITH A *RELIGIOUS FANATIC!* OH, WELL... AT LEAST I HAVEN'T SPOTTED ANY *TROUBLE* ON OUR TRAIL...

"...YET. I CAN'T BELIEVE BOB'S ENEMIES WILL GIVE UP EASILY!"

GALT AND ANOTHER MAN SLIPPED THROUGH OUR NET IN METROPOLIS! IT'S PAINFULLY OBVIOUS THAT OUR FIELD AGENTS *ALONE* ARE INCAPABLE OF TRAILING THAT HERETIC *CULTIST!*

SEQUOIA TECHTRONICS

...WHERE, AFTER A FAILED ATTEMPT TO CONVERT AN AUTO RENTAL AGENT...

U-RENT-IT
-A SEQUOIA ... S COMPANY-

YES, MA'AM... SOON AS YOU CALLED! HAD THAT BABY IN THE JEEP BEFORE THEY EVEN GOT TO THE LOT!

U-RENT-IT
-A SEQUOIA TECHTRONICS COMPANY-

MR. HODGES?

WE'VE GOT THEM, SIR!

CONTINUED NEXT WEEK!

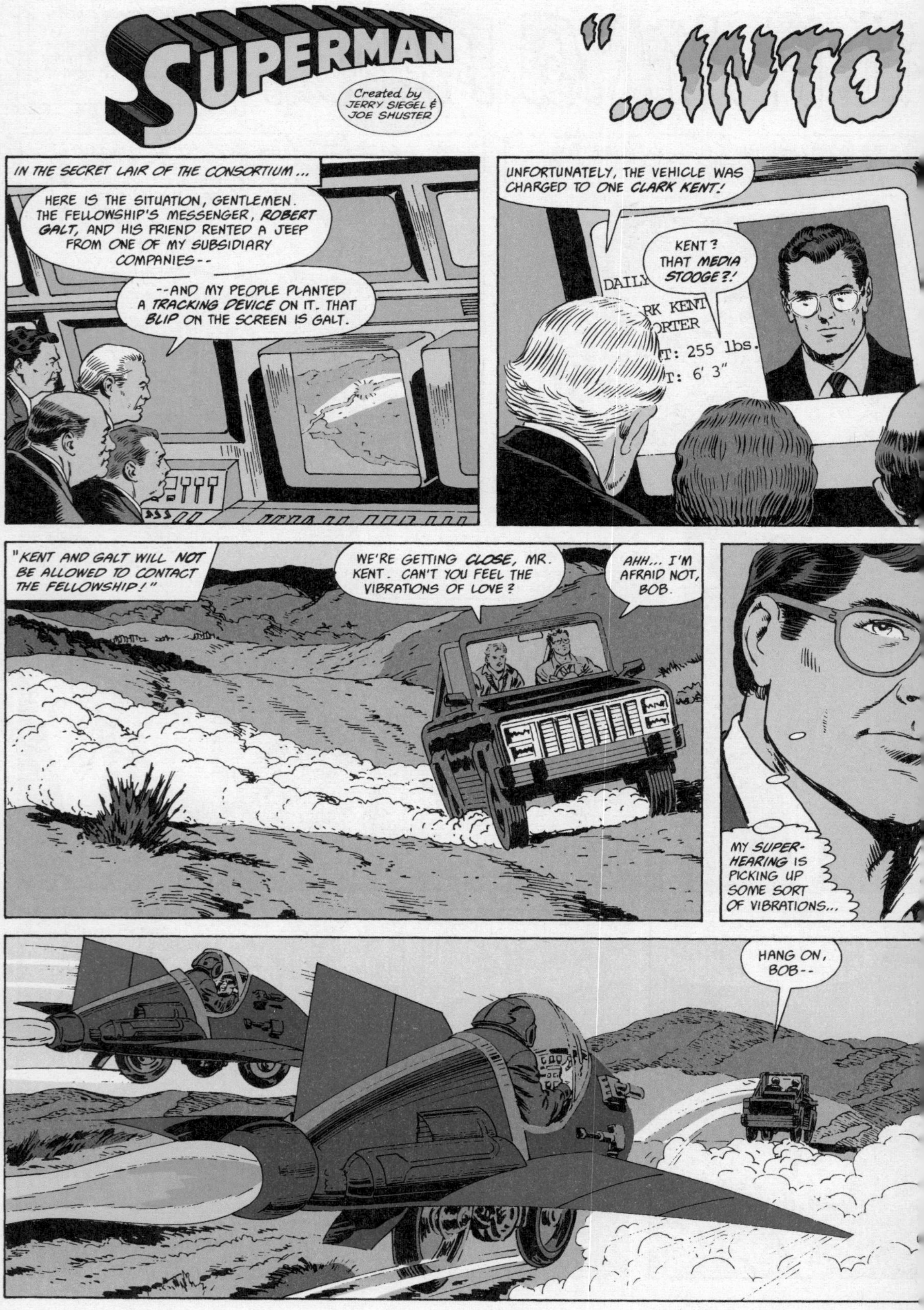
SUPERMAN
Created by JERRY SIEGEL & JOE SHUSTER
"...INTO
IN THE SECRET LAIR OF THE CONSORTIUM...
HERE IS THE SITUATION, GENTLEMEN. THE FELLOWSHIP'S MESSENGER, ROBERT GALT, AND HIS FRIEND RENTED A JEEP FROM ONE OF MY SUBSIDIARY COMPANIES--
--AND MY PEOPLE PLANTED A TRACKING DEVICE ON IT. THAT BLIP ON THE SCREEN IS GALT.
UNFORTUNATELY, THE VEHICLE WAS CHARGED TO ONE CLARK KENT!
KENT? THAT MEDIA STOOGE?!
255 lbs.
6' 3"
"KENT AND GALT WILL NOT BE ALLOWED TO CONTACT THE FELLOWSHIP!"
WE'RE GETTING CLOSE, MR. KENT. CAN'T YOU FEEL THE VIBRATIONS OF LOVE?
AHH... I'M AFRAID NOT, BOB.
MY SUPER-HEARING IS PICKING UP SOME SORT OF VIBRATIONS...
HANG ON, BOB--

THE FIRE!"

ROGER STERN - WRITER
CURT SWAN - PENCILLER
MURPHY ANDERSON - INKER
BILL OAKLEY - LETTERER
TOM ZIUKO - COLORIST
MIKE CARLIN - EDITOR

HIS SYNDICATED COLUMN IS NOTHING BUT AN *ADVERTISE-MENT* FOR *SUPERMAN* -- AN ANTHEM FOR THAT FLYING *ZEALOT!*

THIS CHANGES *EVERYTHING!*

EXACTLY! IF KENT WHIPS UP PUBLIC SYMPATHY FOR THE *FELLOWSHIP*, WE'LL NEVER BE ABLE TO DESTROY THE REST OF THOSE *DEVIL-WORSHIPERS!*

BUT I'VE ALREADY TAKEN *PRECAUTIONS*, GENTLEMEN!

...BUT I DON'T THINK THEY HAVE ANYTHING TO DO WITH *LOVE!*

MR. KENT! WATCH THE ROAD!

--AND STAY *DOWN!!*

CONTINUED NEXT WEEK!

SUPERMAN

Created by
JERRY SIEGEL &
JOE SHUSTER

UNAWARE THAT A HOMING DEVICE PLANTED IN THEIR RENTAL JEEP HAS ALLOWED THEM TO BE FOLLOWED, CLARK KENT AND BOB GALT SUDDENLY FIND THEMSELVES UNDER ATTACK BY AGENTS OF THE CONSORTIUM!

"PANIC

HOW DID THEY FIND US?

I'VE HAD MY EYES PEELED FOR TROUBLE SINCE WE LEFT METROPOLIS!

"IT WOULD BE A LOT SIMPLER IF I COULD HANDLE THIS AS SUPERMAN..."

NICE BIKES, FELLOWS! MIND IF I TAKE A CLOSER LOOK?

KERFLANG

HMMM... FEELS LIKE TITANIUM!

THAT MAKES FOR A NICE LIGHT-WEIGHT FRAME...

IF I SAVE THE DAY AS SUPERMAN, I'LL NEVER CONVINCE BOB THAT I'M NOT A GOD! THERE MUST BE ANOTHER WAY...

IN THE SANDS!"

ROGER STERN – WRITER
CURT SWAN – PENCILLER
MURPHY ANDERSON – INKER
BILL OAKLEY – LETTERER
TOM ZIUKO – COLORIST
MIKE CARLIN – EDITOR

I MUST BE GETTING *SLOPPY!* MY NEGLIGENCE COULD COST BOB HIS *LIFE!*

I CAN'T LET THAT HAPPEN! I HAVE TO GET US OUT OF THIS... SOMEHOW.

I MIGHT BE ABLE TO TAKE OUT THOSE FLYING BIKES WITH MY *HEAT VISION.* BUT WITHOUT KNOWING MORE ABOUT THEIR DESIGN, I MIGHT ALSO BLOW THEM AND THEIR RIDERS TO *KINGDOM COME!*

...BUT IT'S AWFULLY *FRAGILE,* DON'T YOU THINK?

SUPERMAN!

I KNEW YOU WOULDN'T FORSAKE ME! THIS *PROVES* THAT YOU WATCH OVER THOSE OF US WHO WORSHIP YOU!

"*DID I SAY 'SIMPLER'?*"

...AND I'D BETTER THINK OF ONE *FAST!*

MR. KENT-- WE'RE HIT!

KRATOOM

NEXT WEEK: "WIPEOUT!"

SUPERMAN®

Created by
JERRY SIEGEL &
JOE SHUSTER

WHAT HAS GONE BEFORE: REPORTER CLARK KENT (SECRETLY SUPERMAN) HAS JOURNEYED TO CALIFORNIA WITH YOUNG BOB GALT, IN HOPES OF LEARNING MORE ABOUT BOB'S STRANGE SUPERMAN-WORSHIPING FELLOWSHIP. BUT A PAIR OF SUPER-ASSASSINS ARE DETERMINED TO STOP THEM!

THOSE CREEPS ARE TOYING WITH US! THEY PROBABLY PLAN TO BLOW THIS JEEP APART PIECE BY PIECE, UNTIL THEY...

...BOB? WHAT ARE YOU DOING?!

DANGEROUS? ALL RIGHT, I'LL SHOW THEM...

"...METROPOLIS!"

W-WHAT?! W-WHERE ARE WE?

THE BUILDINGS! THEY'RE...GOING AWAY?

SO ARE OUR SKY-BIKES, YOU DOPE! WE'VE BEEN OUT-PSYCHED!

WIPEOUT!

ROGER STERN – WRITER
CURT SWAN – PENCILLER
MURPHY ANDERSON – INKER
BILL OAKLEY – LETTERER
TOM ZIUKO – COLORIST
MIKE CARLIN – EDITOR

I'M PRAYING TO SUPERMAN... THAT I MIGHT LIVE TO SHOW THE FELLOWSHIP ELDERS THIS HORRIBLE TABLEAU!

SHOW--? THAT'S IT! BOB, YOUR POWER CAN SAVE US!

IT CAN? BUT, MR. KENT, I CAN ONLY CREATE IMAGES OF THINGS I HAVE EXPERIENCED! I DON'T SEE HOW--!

BOB, JUST USE THE POWER! SHOW THOSE AIRBORNE BIKERS SOMETHING BIG AND DANGEROUS!

NO TIME TO SWERVE -- WE'RE GONNA CRASH!

DAILY PLANET

BAIL OUT!!

I DID IT, MR. KENT! WE'RE SAFE!

FOR NOW, MAYBE. BUT WE STILL DON'T KNOW HOW THOSE TWO FOUND US... OR WHO SENT THEM!

I HAVE TO GET SOME ANSWERS OUT OF THOSE TWO BEFORE THEIR BOSSES STRIKE AGAIN!

CONTINUED NEXT WEEK!

SUPERMAN®

Created by
JERRY SIEGEL &
JOE SHUSTER

LAST WEEK: WITH A LITTLE COACHING FROM *CLARK KENT,* SUPERMAN-WORSHIPER *BOB GALT* UTILIZED HIS IMAGE-CASTING POWER TO STOP TWO *CONSORTIUM* ASSASSINS!

IF I CAN SLIP AWAY FROM BOB FOR JUST A MINUTE, I MIGHT BE ABLE TO GET SOME *ANSWERS* OUT OF THOSE TWO... AS *SUPERMAN!*

BUT BEFORE KENT CAN MAKE HIS MOVE...

...THE *DESERT SANDS* MAKE *THEIRS!*

HOME, MR. KENT! THIS IS THE *SECRET SANCTUARY* OF THE *FELLOWSHIP!*

SO! THE EARTH HAS BROUGHT ME AN *INFIDEL* AND A *TRAITOR!*

YOU WERE SUPPOSED TO SUMMON *SUPERMAN* TO OUR AID, ROBERT! INSTEAD, YOU BRING US THIS... THIS *STRANGER!*

DOESN'T THE SECURITY OF THE FELLOWSHIP MEAN *ANYTHING* TO YOU? DON'T YOU REALIZE THAT WE ARE AT *WAR?*

THIS WAS THE MESSAGE THAT APPEARED BEFORE MY EYES... BURNED INTO A COMMON POSTER BY THE HOLY POWER OF HEAT VISION!

TRUST KENT

GREAT KRYPTON!

FORGIVE MY MISTRUST, BLESSED ONE, BUT THE FELLOWSHIP FACES *GRAVE THREATS* FROM THE OUTSIDE WORLD! I AM MOTHER TIERRA ...PLEASE, COME GRACE MY FELLOW ELDERS WITH YOUR PRESENCE!

IT WOULD BE MY PLEASURE... AH... HOLY MOTHER. THERE IS SO MUCH I WISH TO LEARN ABOUT YOUR GROUP.

JOURNEY'S END

ROGER STERN — WRITER
CURT SWAN — PENCILLER
MURPHY ANDERSON — INKER
BILL OAKLEY — LETTERER
TOM ZIUKO — COLORIST
MIKE CARLIN — EDITOR

WHAT IN THE--? *BOB,* GRAB HOLD!

DON'T BE ALARMED, MR. KENT! SEE HOW THE SANDS APPEAR *ALIVE?* THIS MUST BE *MOTHER TIERRA'S* DOING! SHE'S DRAWING US INTO HER EXALTED PRESENCE!

MOTHER *WHO?* WHAT IS GOING ON, *BOB?* WHERE ARE WE?

M-MOTHER TIERRA! HEAR ME OUT! THIS MAN, CLARK KENT, IS *BLESSED!* I KNOW! *SUPERMAN* HIMSELF SENT ME A SIGN!

USE YOUR POWER, THEN... IT CANNOT LIE! SHOW ME WHAT YOU SAW!

MEANWHILE, IN THE SECRET LAIR OF THE CONSORTIUM...

THE TRAIL ENDS HERE. I KNOW IT SOUNDS CRAZY, SIR, BUT OUR INSTRUMENTS INDICATE THAT THE GROUND... WELL... *SWALLOWED* THEM UP!

OF COURSE! THE FELLOWSHIP HIDEOUT MUST BE BENEATH THE DESERT FLOOR! WE'VE *FOUND* THEM!

NOW WE CAN SEND THOSE *DEVIL-WORSHIPERS* STRAIGHT TO *HELL!*

CONTINUED NEXT WEEK!

SUPERMAN® THE POWER

Created by
JERRY SIEGEL &
JOE SHUSTER

AS THE FORCES OF THE *CONSORTIUM* RUSH TO ENGAGE AND EXTERMINATE THE *SUPERMAN-WORSHIPING FELLOWSHIP*...

YOUR SUPER-SENSES SERVE YOU WELL, *LISTENER!*

FELLOW ELDERS, I GIVE YOU *CLARK KENT*... AN APOSTLE RICH IN THE GLORY OF SUPERMAN!

BLESSED BE!

DO YOU SEE? THE POWERS OF WHICH WE ALWAYS *DREAMED* HAVE BEEN GRANTED US! WE CAN MAKE THE EARTH QUAKE OR CHANGE THE COURSE OF MIGHTY RIVERS... ALL BECAUSE *SUPERMAN* HEARS OUR PRAYERS!

THERE'S SOMETHING *STRANGE* AT WORK HERE... SOME UNFAMILIAR VARIETY OF... *RADIATION?*

SOME *EXTERNAL FORCE* IS GENERATING THEIR POWERS, ALL RIGHT... BUT IT CERTAINLY ISN'T *ME!* THAT ENERGY PULSE IS COMING FROM *ABOVE!* IF I CAN JUST TRACE IT TO ITS SOURCE...

FROM BEYOND!

ROGER STERN – WRITER
CURT SWAN – PENCILLER
MURPHY ANDERSON – INKER
BILL OAKLEY – LETTERER
TOM ZIUKO – COLORIST
MIKE CARLIN – EDITOR

...CLARK KENT GETS A RARE GLIMPSE OF THE HIDDEN REFUGE OF THAT STRANGE CULT.

DO NOT LOOK SO AMAZED, MR. KENT! OUR RELIGION IS NOT THE FIRST TO BE DRIVEN UNDERGROUND BY VIOLENT OPPRESSORS!

NO, MOTHER TIERRA! BUT NOT MANY WERE LITERALLY SHELTERED UNDERGROUND... AND NONE HAD A PRIESTESS WHO COULD MAKE THE EARTH MOVE!

WE ELDERS CAN WORK MIRACLES, IT IS TRUE! BUT ONLY THROUGH THE GRACE OF SUPERMAN!

IS IT TRUE WHAT I HEARD, TIERRA? IS THIS MAN INDEED A TRUSTED FRIEND OF OUR SAVIOR?

THIS IS BUT A FRACTION OF THE FAITHFUL! THE OTHERS HAVE SCATTERED TO THEIR OWN HIDEAWAYS... THOSE WHO WERE NOT MURDERED IN THE ATTACK ON OUR COMMUNE.

THOSE WHO REMAIN HERE ARE CALLED "ELDERS" FOR THEIR INNER STRENGTHS HAVE MATURED THROUGH MEDITATION AND THE INVOCATION OF THE HOLY NAME!

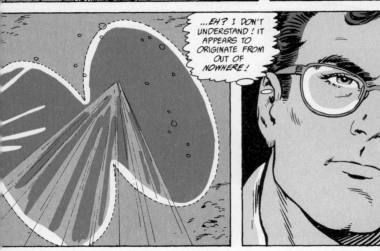

...EH? I DON'T UNDERSTAND! IT APPEARS TO ORIGINATE FROM OUT OF NOWHERE!

IF THESE CULTISTS ARE AS SINCERE AS THEY SEEM, THEN SOMEONE VERY DANGEROUS IS MANIPULATING THEM...

...WITH A TECHNOLOGY AS POWERFUL AS ANY I'VE EVER FACED!

CONTINUED NEXT WEEK!

SUPERMAN

Created by
JERRY SIEGEL &
JOE SHUSTER

"POINT

IN THE HIDDEN CALIFORNIA SANCTUARY OF THE FELLOWSHIP...

WITH YOUR OWN EYES, MR. KENT, YOU HAVE SEEN HOW WORSHIPING SUPERMAN HAS ENDOWED US WITH GREAT POWERS. BUT YOU HAVE HAD A LONG JOURNEY... PLEASE, REST! AND REFLECT ON THOSE POWERS...

...THEY COULD BE YOURS!

THESE CULTISTS *DO* HAVE SOME PRETTY IMPRESSIVE POWERS... BUT THEY DIDN'T GET THEM FROM SUPERMAN! THE ENERGY BEHIND THEM ORIGINATES FROM SOMEWHERE IN *SPACE*...

...AND FROM THIS ANGLE IT APPEARS THAT THERE'S MORE THAN ONE POWER BEAM. INTERESTING ...LET'S SEE WHERE THE OTHER ONE LEADS...

MR. KENT? I DON'T WANT TO DISTURB YOU, BUT I THOUGHT YOU MIGHT BE HUNGRY AND...

MR. KENT? WHERE'D HE GO?

"DEMON"? IS THAT WHY THEY'RE ATTACKING THE FELLOWSHIP WORSHIPERS? THEY THINK I'M SOME KIND OF *DEVIL*?

ONLY IN CALIFORNIA!

FIRE!

66

BLANK"

ROGER STERN – WRITER
CURT SWAN – PENCILER
MURPHY ANDERSON – INKER
BILL OAKLEY – LETTERER
TOM ZIUKO – COLORIST
MIKE CARLIN – EDITOR

...GOOD LORD! RIGHT TO A *SMALL ARMY!* AND IT LOOKS LIKE IT'S HEADED THIS WAY!

WITH LUCK, NO ONE WILL NOTICE THAT CLARK KENT IS MISSING!

RIGHT NOW I'M MORE CONCERNED BY THE FACT THAT *BOTH* THE FELLOWSHIP AND THEIR HIGH-TECH ATTACKERS ARE RECEIVING POWER FROM THE *SAME SOURCE.* WHO -- OR WHAT -- IS FEEDING IT TO THEM?

I WONDER IF I'VE ANY HOPE OF GETTING THE ANSWERS FROM THESE TROOPS?

RED ALERT! IT'S THE *DEMON* HIMSELF!

EEVAARGH!

NEXT WEEK: "HOLY WAR!"

SUPERMAN

Created by
JERRY SIEGEL &
JOE SHUSTER

LAST WEEK: CLARK KENT SLIPPED AWAY FROM THE SECRET SANCTUARY OF THE FELLOWSHIP TO STOP AN IMPENDING ATTACK BY CONSORTIUM TROOPS... AS *SUPERMAN!*

MOTHER TIERRA! MR. KENT IS GONE-- VANISHED!

LISTENER, CAN YOUR *SUPER-HEARING* LOCATE OUR GUEST?

I... I DON'T HEAR MR. KENT ANYWHERE, BUT... VERY CLOSE... THERE IS THE DIN OF *WAR MACHINES!*

...THE OBJECT OF HER REVERENCE HAS ALREADY FACED THE FELLOWSHIP'S ENEMIES!

DON'T KNOW... WHAT KIND OF ENERGY... THESE TROOPS ARE USING... BUT IT SURE... HURTS!

SAVE YOURSELVES! IT'S THE *BEAST OF THE APOCALYPSE!*

OH, *SHUT UP!*

I SHOULD BE ABLE TO MAKE SHORT WORK OF THIS BUNCH, BARRING ANY UNFORESEEN...

...COMPLICA- TIONS?

HOLY WAR

ROGER STERN – WRITER
CURT SWAN – PENCILLER
MURPHY ANDERSON – INKER
BILL OAKLEY – LETTERER
TOM ZIUKO – COLORIST
MIKE CARLIN – EDITOR

SO, OUR ENEMIES HAVE RETURNED... NO DOUBT TO FINISH SLAUGHTERING US FOR OUR BELIEF IN THE *DIVINITY* OF SUPERMAN!

THE LAST TIME, WE AWAITED THEM *MEEKLY!* BUT THIS TIME...

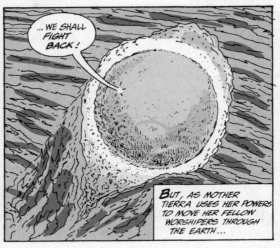

...WE SHALL *FIGHT BACK!*

BUT, AS MOTHER TIERRA USES HER POWERS TO MOVE HER FELLOW WORSHIPERS THROUGH THE EARTH...

THE *POWER* OF THEIR ATTACK TOOK ME BY SURPRISE, BUT IT WON'T AGAIN!

KRA-VWHOOSH

OH, NO!

MAKE *WAR*, BROTHERS AND SISTERS...

...FOR THE *GLORY* OF SUPERMAN!

CONTINUED NEXT WEEK!

SUPERMAN®

Created by
JERRY SIEGEL &
JOE SHUSTER

TWO MYSTERIOUS GROUPS-- ONE THAT WORSHIPS SUPERMAN, AND ONE THAT REVILES HIM -- COLLIDE ON A DESERT BATTLEFIELD!

STRIKE AT THE FAITHLESS INFIDELS, BROTHERS AND SISTERS! STRIKE IN THE NAME OF OUR POWER-GRANTING LORD... *SUPERMAN!*

THEY DIDN'T HEAR ME... EVEN IF THEY HAD, I DOUBT THEY'D HAVE LISTENED! THEY'RE COMPLETELY OUT OF CONTROL! THEY'LL *KILL* EACH OTHER--

--OWW!-- AND I CAN'T EVEN GET IN THERE TO TRY TO STOP THEM! WHOEVER'S FEEDING THIS *ENERGY* TO THEM MUST BE TURNING UP THE JUICE! THE POWER'S INCREASING *EXPONENTIALLY!*

...THE MAN OF STEEL CHARGES INTO THE THRESHOLD OF SPACE!

I STILL CAN'T SENSE ANY TRACE OF THE POWER BEAM'S SOURCE... IT MUST BE COMING FROM SOME SORT OF *INVISIBLE SATELLITE!* I JUST HAVE TO HOPE THAT A GOOD SOLID BLOW CAN KNOCK IT OUT OF...

BOOM

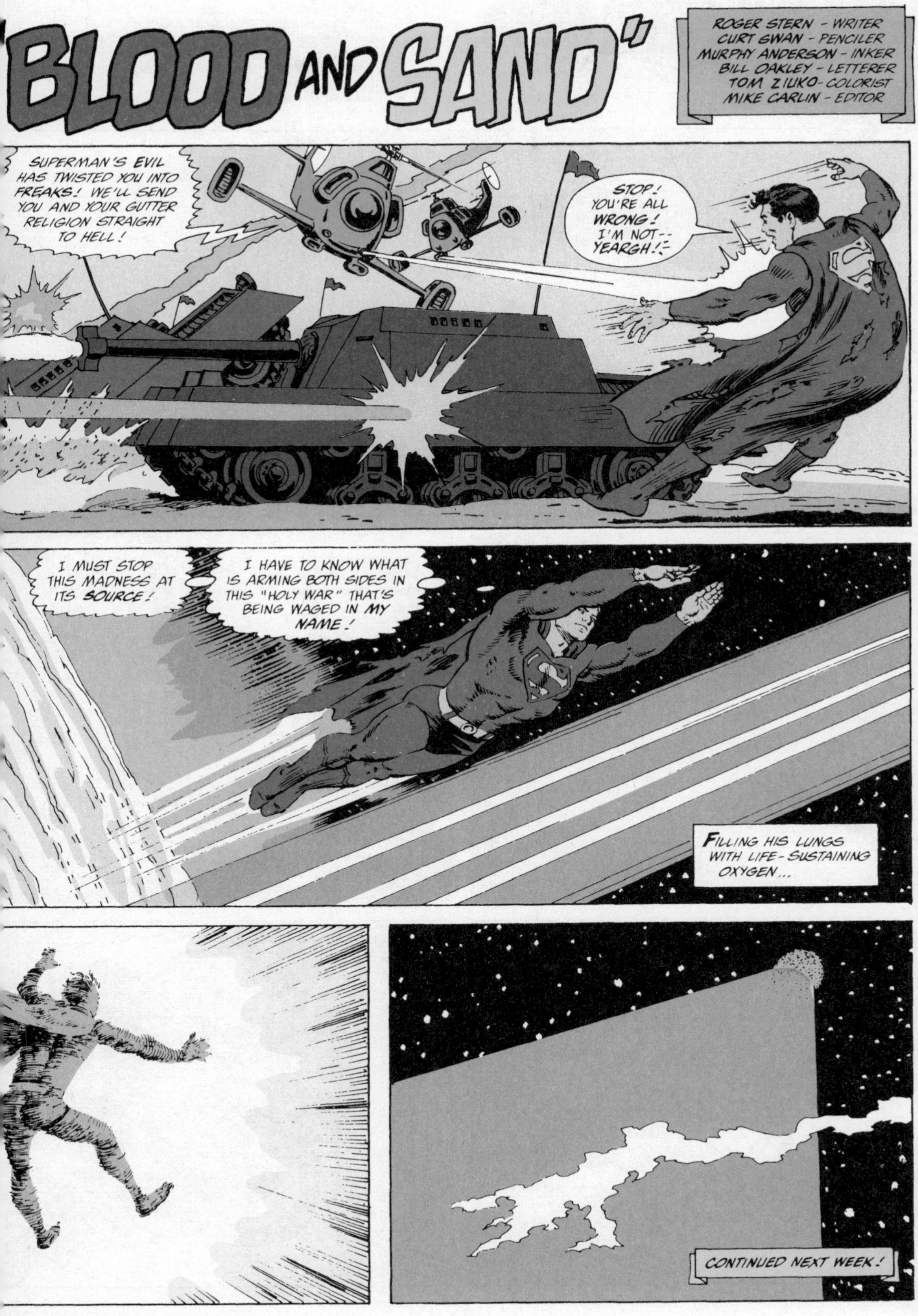
"BLOOD AND SAND"
ROGER STERN - WRITER
CURT SWAN - PENCILER
MURPHY ANDERSON - INKER
BILL OAKLEY - LETTERER
TOM ZIUKO - COLORIST
MIKE CARLIN - EDITOR
SUPERMAN'S EVIL HAS TWISTED YOU INTO FREAKS! WE'LL SEND YOU AND YOUR GUTTER RELIGION STRAIGHT TO HELL!
STOP! YOU'RE ALL WRONG! I'M NOT-- YEARGH!
I MUST STOP THIS MADNESS AT ITS SOURCE!
I HAVE TO KNOW WHAT IS ARMING BOTH SIDES IN THIS "HOLY WAR" THAT'S BEING WAGED IN MY NAME!
FILLING HIS LUNGS WITH LIFE-SUSTAINING OXYGEN...
CONTINUED NEXT WEEK!

SUPERMAN®

Created by
JERRY SIEGEL &
JOE SHUSTER

RUSHING TO SHUT DOWN A SPACE-BORN ENERGY BEAM THAT POWERS TWO WARRING GROUPS ON EARTH, SUPERMAN IS SWEPT FROM THE FACE OF THE UNIVERSE BY A MYSTERIOUS FORCE!

WH-WHERE AM I?

MUST HAVE BEEN... TELEPORTED SOMEWHERE... SHOCK KNOCKED MOST OF THE BREATH OUT OF ME.

...AND WHATEVER HAPPENS... I'M GOING TO DO IT...

...BEFORE THOSE POOR, DELUDED IDIOTS... BACK ON EARTH... WIPE EACH OTHER OUT!

WHATEVER THIS THING'S MADE OF... IT'S NOT... THAT TOUGH...

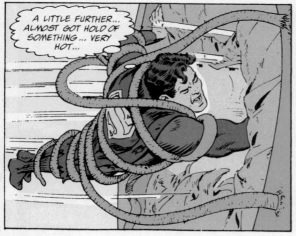

A LITTLE FURTHER... ALMOST GOT HOLD OF SOMETHING... VERY HOT...

DID IT!

"BREATHLESS!"

ROGER STERN – WRITER
CURT SWAN – PENCILLER
MURPHY ANDERSON – INKER
BILL OAKLEY – LETTERER
TOM ZIUKO – COLORIST
MIKE CARLIN – EDITOR

NO AIR HERE... WHEREVER HERE IS!

THAT MACHINE--! I CAME HERE TO STOP... THAT MACHINE...

?!?!

LUNGS FEEL... AS IF THEY'RE... ON FIRE!

GOT TO... IGNORE THE PAIN...

NOW... GOT TO FIND MY WAY OUT OF HERE... GOT TO FIND AIR FAST...

...OR... I'M... DEAD...

CONTINUED NEXT WEEK ?

73

 **"POWER**

IN THE SECRET LAIR OF THE CONSORTIUM...

DAMN! OUR ASSAULT TEAM HAD JUST ATTACKED THOSE SUPERMAN-WORSHIPING HEATHENS... OF ALL THE TIMES TO LOSE TRANSMISSION!

YOU HAVE LOST *FAR MORE* THAN THAT!

"EVEN NOW, HE ATTEMPTS TO ESCAPE MY INTERDIMENSIONAL PORTAL...

"...FOR WHATEVER GOOD IT WILL DO HIM.

COWARDS! THEY'RE BUGGING OUT ON US!

I DON'T CARE...

... I CAME HERE TO ACE SUPERMAN - CULTISTS, AND THAT'S JUST WHAT I AIM TO DO!

FAILURE!"

ROGER STERN – WRITER
CURT SWAN – PENCILLER
MURPHY ANDERSON – INKER
BILL OAKLEY – LETTERER
TOM ZIUKO – COLORIST
MIKE CARLIN – EDITOR

WHAT?! WH-WHO THE DEVIL ARE YOU?

YOU MIGHT CALL ME YOUR SILENT PARTNER! FOR MANY MONTHS, I HAVE SECRETLY SUPPLIED THE ENERGY WHICH POWERS YOUR WAR MACHINES...

"...THAT ENERGY HAS BEEN CUT OFF, ITS GENERATOR DESTROYED BY THE BEING YOU LOATHE. YES, BY SUPERMAN... BUT ONLY AT GREAT COST TO HIM..."

LUNGS ABOUT TO BURST! MUST... FIND... AIR!

"YOUR TROOPS, MEANWHILE, ARE LEFT MANNING WEAPONS AS POWERLESS AS THE ENEMIES THEY FACE."

OUR POWERS... THEY'RE GONE! HAS SUPERMAN FORSAKEN US?

'UD

YOU'RE RIGHT, SEELY! LONG AS WE'RE STUCK HERE, WE MIGHT AS WELL MAKE THE MOST OF IT!

I'D RATHER DIE A MARTYR THAN LIVE WITH YOUR EVIL!

HAPPY TO OBLIGE, BOY!

CONTINUED NEXT WEEK!

SUPERMAN®

Created by
JERRY SIEGEL &
JOE SHUSTER

RENDERED POWERLESS BY SUPERMAN'S DESTRUCTION OF A MYSTERIOUS ENERGY GENERATOR, THE CONSORTIUM AND THE FELLOWSHIP CONTINUE THEIR BATTLE!

SUPERMAN!

KRAANCH

SUPERMAN, YOU SAVED MY LIFE... *AGAIN!* YOU SAVED ALL OF US!

UH... ARE YOU ALL RIGHT?

NEED A MINUTE... TO FINISH CATCHING MY BREATH, BOB. WHERE I JUST CAME FROM ...THERE WASN'T ANY AIR!

ROBERT GALT, HOW *DARE* YOU ADDRESS OUR SAVIOR IN SUCH FAMILIAR TONES?! YOU BRING SHAME UNTO OUR ENTIRE FELLOWSHIP!

FOOLS!!

THAT VOICE!

OF COURSE, HE HAD TO BE THE ONE BEHIND THIS MADNESS! ONLY HE WOULD HAVE THE *POWER*...

⊣E FACE AND THE VOICE!"

ROGER STERN – WRITER
CURT SWAN – PENCILLER
MURPHY ANDERSON – INKER
BILL OAKLEY – LETTERER
TOM ZIUKO – COLORIST
MIKE CARLIN – EDITOR

GOT BACK...TO EARTH... JUST IN TIME. IT FIGURES... THAT THESE FANATICS... WOULD STILL BE FIGHTING!

I'VE HAD... ENOUGH... OF YOUR... HOLY WAR!

THE DEMON HAS RETURNED! RUN FOR YOUR LIVES!

NOT AGAIN! I'M TIRED OF THIS MISGUIDED HERO WORSHIP!

I'D BETTER SEE TO ROUNDING UP THOSE ERRANT TROOPS BEFORE I SAY SOMETHING I'LL REGRET!

LOOK, CHILDREN! THE HOLY ONE ASCENDS! PRAISE THE MIRACLE YOU'VE SEEN THIS DAY!

SUPERMAN IS NO GOD! NOR IS HE A DEVIL!

I KNOW... FOR I AM BOTH!

NEXT WEEK: THE POWER OF DARKSEID!

SUPERMAN

Created by JERRY SIEGEL & JOE SHUSTER

THE POWER OF

DARKSEID! I SHOULD HAVE SEEN YOUR HANDIWORK IN THIS!

W-WHO IS THAT, SUPER-MAN?

SOMEONE BEYOND YOUR KEN, LITTLE BUG!

SUFFICE IT TO SAY, I RULE APOKOLIPS, A DISTANT SPHERE OF UNRELENTING TERRORS.

I BECAME INTRIGUED BY THE WAY CERTAIN HUMAN LIVES COULD BE CONSUMED BY FANATICISM!

YOUR GROUP, FOR INSTANCE, IDOLIZED SUPERMAN ... WHILE YOUR OPPOSITE NUMBER FEARED AND LOATHED HIM.

THE MURDERS WERE THE WORK OF THESE GIFTED MEN, WHO LED THE ANTI-SUPERMAN FORCES! THEY CALLED THEMSELVES "THE CONSORTIUM."

THIS ONE -- CALLED "HODGES"-- WAS MORE THAN WILLING TO UTILIZE ANY MEANS TO FURTHER HIS OWN ENDS! HE AND HIS COHORTS SHOULD PRO-VIDE MY TECHNICIANS WITH MANY DIVERTING HOURS OF STUDY--

DARKSEID!

ROGER STERN – WRITER
CURT SWAN – PENCILLER
MURPHY ANDERSON – INKER
BILL OAKLEY – LETTERER
TOM ZIUKO – COLORIST
MIKE CARLIN – EDITOR

ONE DAY MY RULE WILL EXTEND TO EARTH ...I SHALL HOLD DOMINION OVER ALL *LIFE* THROUGHOUT THIS *UNIVERSE!*

BUT BEFORE THAT DAY CAN BECOME REALITY, I MUST SUBVERT THE HIDDEN FACETS OF THE HUMAN MIND THAT MIGHT GENERATE THE DESIRE FOR FREEDOM!

OVER MY DEAD--!

DO NOT *TEMPT* ME, SUPERMAN.

I NEEDED TO DO NO MORE THAN PLANT *SUGGESTIONS* IN A FEW KEY MINDS..., AND SUPPLY BOTH GROUPS WITH EVER-INCREASING *POWER.* THE HOLY WAR YOU FOUGHT IN RESPONSE MORE THAN FULFILLED MY EXPECTATIONS!

YOU MONSTER--!

DO YOU HAVE ANY IDEA HOW MANY *LIVES* WERE LOST TO YOUR LITTLE "SCIENCE PROJECT?"

THIRTY-FOUR. BUT I CANNOT TAKE ALL OF THE CREDIT.

--IN THE "SCREAM-CENTERS" OF APOKOLIPS!!!

DARKSEID, NO!!

AAIIEEEEEEE

CONCLUDED NEXT WEEK!

SUPERMAN

Created by
JERRY SIEGEL &
JOE SHUSTER

IN THE AFTERMATH OF A BIZARRE HOLY WAR, THE POWER BEHIND THE CONFLICT-- *DARKSEID, LORD OF APOKOLIPS*-- HAS TAKEN *JOHN HODGES* AND HIS FELLOW *CONSORTIUM* LEADERS PRISONER.

WHATEVER THOSE MEN HAVE DONE, DARKSEID, THEY BELONG HERE ON EARTH! RELEASE THEM, OR-- *≠WUHN!≠*

I DID NOT COME TO *NEGOTIATE*, SUPERMAN! I CAME ONLY TO SEE MY LITTLE EXPERIMENT TO ITS CONCLUSION!

I WANTED THE PEOPLE WHO WORSHIPED YOU TO WITNESS *TRUE POWER!* AND I WANT *YOU* TO REMEMBER THIS: THE NEXT TIME YOU ARE BEDEVILED BY CIRCUM-STANCES BEYOND YOUR KEN...

FORGIVE ME, HOLY ONE, BUT THOSE "HELPLESS MEN" HAD HALF OF OUR FOLLOWING *MURDERED!* SURELY, THEY DESERVE THEIR FATE?

DON'T CALL ME "*HOLY ONE!*" DIDN'T YOU *HEAR* HIM?

SUPERMAN, YOUR FRIEND-- *CLARK KENT* --DISAPPEARED BEFORE THE BATTLE.

DON'T WORRY ABOUT KENT... I SENT HIM OFF TO ARRANGE TRANSPORT FOR YOU! JUST WAIT HERE.

OH, BOB...BOB! I FEEL AS IF HE'S RIPPED AWAY A PIECE OF MY SOUL!

"THE POWER WITHIN"

MIKE CARLIN — EDITOR
TOM ZIUKO — COLORIST
BILL OAKLEY — LETTERER
MURPHY ANDERSON — INKER
CURT SWAN — PENCILLER
ROGER STERN — WRITER
—with special thanks to
TOM PEYER!

...THINK OF ME! HAHAHAHAHA!

GONE! I COULDN'T STOP HIM FROM TAKING THOSE HELPLESS MEN!

I HEARD THE EVIL ONE TRY TO TEST OUR FAITH, BUT—

LISTEN! IT WAS DARKSEID WHO GRANTED YOU SUPER-POWERS, NOT ME! IN RETURN, YOU FORFEITED THE GREATEST POWER OF ALL—YOUR ABILITY TO THINK FOR YOURSELVES!

YOU HAVE A RESPONSIBILITY TO USE THAT POWER. DON'T WORSHIP ME... FOR ALL MY ABILITIES, I'M NO GOD. I'M NOT ALL KNOWING, AND I'M NOT IMMORTAL.

SOMEDAY, I WILL DIE, TOO... DON'T WAIT UNTIL THEN TO TAKE CHARGE OF YOUR LIVES. YOU DON'T NEED SUPER-POWERS TO MAKE A DIFFERENCE IN THE WORLD! THINK ABOUT THAT.

YOU'RE WRONG, TIERRA. HE JUST TOOK OUR SOULS FROM DARKSEID...

"... AND GAVE THEM BACK TO US!"

SUPERMAN.

Created by
JERRY SIEGEL &
JOE SHUSTER

"AN EYE

A MAJOR STORY DISRUPTS THE DAILY ROUTINE OF THE *PLANET* NEWSROOM ...

WHAT'S THE LATEST ON THAT *SUICIDE* BOMBING, LOIS?

THE *DEATH TOLL'S* UP TO 16 -- AND QURAC IS CLAIMING CREDIT!

WHY THOSE *MISERABLE--!*

THREE OF THE DEAD ARE *AMERICANS!* WHY ISN'T ANY-BODY DOING *SOMETHING* ABOUT IT?

IT WASN'T SO LONG AGO THAT SUPERMAN TOOK OUT THEIR ENTIRE *AIR FORCE.* IF I WAS HIM, I'D GO BACK AND PULL THE *LEGS* OFF EVERY LAST *QURACI!*

"... I MIGHT AS WELL GO TO *LUNCH!*"

WHAT'D I TELL YOU, MARTY? HE'S *OPEN!*

NOT FOR *LONG!*

WHY DO I *BOTHER* OPENING TODAY? EVERY TIME THERE IS A TERRORIST ATTACK, I SEE NO CUSTOMERS FOR *WEEKS!*

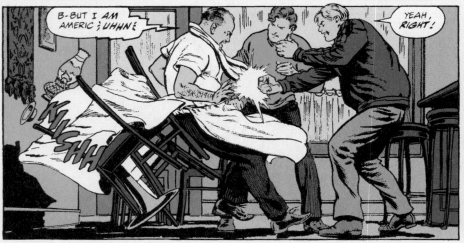

B-BUT I *AM* AMERIC; UHHN;

YEAH, *RIGHT!*

MARTY, YA STARTED A *FIRE!*

82

FOR AN EYE"

ROGER STERN — WRITER
CURT SWAN — PENCILER
MURPHY ANDERSON — INKER
BILL OAKLEY — LETTERER
TOM ZIUKO — COLORIST
MIKE CARLIN — EDITOR
Special thanks to TOM PEYER

GEORGE!

I KNOW YOU'RE ANGRY, GEORGE — SO AM I! BUT YOU CAN'T HOLD AN ENTIRE PEOPLE RESPONSIBLE FOR THE ACTIONS OF AN UNELECTED GOVERNMENT!

BULL, KENT!

AN EYE FOR AN EYE, I SAY! THEY KILL OUR PEOPLE, WE KILL THEIRS!

NO SENSE IN ARGUING WITH SOMEONE WHO WON'T LISTEN TO REASON...

WRONG, Q-RAT!

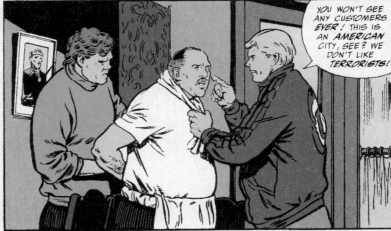

YOU WON'T SEE ANY CUSTOMERS EVER! THIS IS AN AMERICAN CITY, SEE? WE DON'T LIKE TERRORISTS!

OKAY, OKAY! JUST GIVE ME ONE MORE SHOT AT THIS CREEP!

CHUD

AWRIGHT, COME ON! LET'S GET OUT OF HERE!

CONTINUED NEXT WEEK!

THIS IS TERRIBLE! IF ONLY I HADN'T BEEN TIED UP OUT IN CALIFORNIA, MAYBE I COULD'VE DONE SOMETHING ABOUT... EH?

WHAT'S THAT SMELL?

DAILY PLANET

QURACI BOMB KILLS 3 YANKS

SMOKE!

LAMP OIL... COTTON FIBERS... PARTICLE BOARD! COMING FROM ABOUT TWO BLOCKS WEST OF HERE, JUDGING BY THE WIND.

IT'S ALL RIGHT! HELP IS HERE!

S-SUPERMAN! ⸘KOFF⸘ MY RES-TAURANT--!

I'LL GO CALL 911, MR. SUPER-MAN!

GOOD.

NOW, SIR... TWO BOYS ATTACKED YOU?

YES ⸘KOFF⸘ THEY SAID THE QURACI BOMBING WAS MY FAULT! THEY SAID I WAS NOT AN AMERICAN!

BUT I AM AMERICAN! FIND THEM FOR ME, SUPERMAN... I WANT THEM TO KNOW THAT!

THERE'S SMOKE...

ROGER STERN - WRITER
CURT SWAN - PENCILLER
MURPHY ANDERSON - INKER
BILL OAKLEY - LETTERER
TOM ZIUKO - COLORIST
MIKE CARLIN - EDITOR
Special Thanks to TOM PEYER

THIS IS ORDINARILY A JOB FOR THE *FIRE DEPARTMENT,* BUT I KNOW SOMEONE WHO CAN GET THERE EVEN *FASTER!*

¿KOFF- KOFF¿ *HELP... SOMEBODY...* ¿KOFF¿

T-TWO BOYS... ¿KAFF- KAFF¿ THEY COME IN HERE... THEY HIT ME...

...THEN *THIS!*

TELL ME *OUTSIDE!*

THEY SHOULDN'T BE *TOO HARD* TO SPOT, IF THEY WERE ON *FOOT--*

"-- THEY COULDN'T HAVE GONE *FAR!* "

OKAY, *LOU--* STOP ALREADY! TAKE IT *EASY!*

NO ONE SPOTTED US... *NOTHIN'* TO WORRY ABOUT!

CONCLUDED NEXT WEEK!

SUPERMAN.

Created by
JERRY SIEGEL &
JOE SHUSTER

S-SUPERMAN?!

THERE'S A VERY AGITATED GENTLEMAN ABOUT SIX BLOCKS FROM HERE. IT SEEMS HIS *RESTAURANT* WAS NEARLY GUTTED BY FIRE... WITH HIM IN IT!

I THINK HE'D LIKE TO TALK TO YOU.

OH GAWD... OH GAWD...

N-NOT SO *FAST,* SUPERMAN! PLEASE, I THINK I'M GONNA--!

DO YOU RECOGNIZE THESE TWO, SIR?

YES! THEY *BEAT* ME... SET MY *BUSINESS* ON FIRE!

NO, SUPERMAN! IT IS *NOT* MY GOVERNMENT! I FLED THAT CURSED DICTATORSHIP! I TOLD YOU... I AM AN *AMERICAN* NOW!

YA AIN'T A *REAL* AMERICAN! DAMN IMMIGRANTS... YA KEEP LOUSING UP THE COUNTRY!

JUST A MINUTE...

WE ARE A NATION OF IMMIGRANTS! IF YOU GO BACK ENOUGH GENERATIONS, WE ALL CAME FROM SOMEWHERE ELSE!

MY FATHER SENT ME TO EARTH, THAT I MIGHT ESCAPE A DYING WORLD DESTROYED BY THE HATE OF TERRORISTS! THAT DOESN'T MAKE ME ANY MORE OR LESS AMERICAN THAN THIS MAN... OR YOU!

TICE FOR ALL

ROGER STERN – WRITER
CURT SWAN – PENCILLER
MURPHY ANDERSON – INKER
BILL OAKLEY – LETTERER
TOM ZIUKO – COLORIST
MIKE CARLIN – EDITOR
with special thanks to
TOM PEYER

T-TO *US?* W-W-WHY? WE DON'T KNOW WHAT YOU'RE TALKIN' ABOUT!

GEEZ, YOU'RE A LOUSY LIAR!

HEY, COME ON, MAN! THE GEEK WAS *QURACI*... WE WERE JUST DOIN' OUR PATRIOTIC DUTY!

WILL YOU SHUT UP?

HECK, *YOU* WIPED OUT QURAC'S *AIR FORCE!* WE'RE JUST, LIKE, FINISHIN' THE JOB YOU STARTED!

IT'S ALL RIGHT, MR. SADRA... THE POLICE ARE ON THEIR WAY!

I DON'T *BELIEVE* THIS! YOU'RE REALLY SIDIN' WITH THIS *QURACI*?! THEY'RE NOTHIN' BUT *TERRORISTS!*

THIS MAN IS NOT TO BLAME FOR THE POLICIES OF HIS GOVERNMENT.

THINK ABOUT THAT... PLEASE.

I DON'T WANT TO LOSE ANOTHER WORLD TO HATRED!

The End

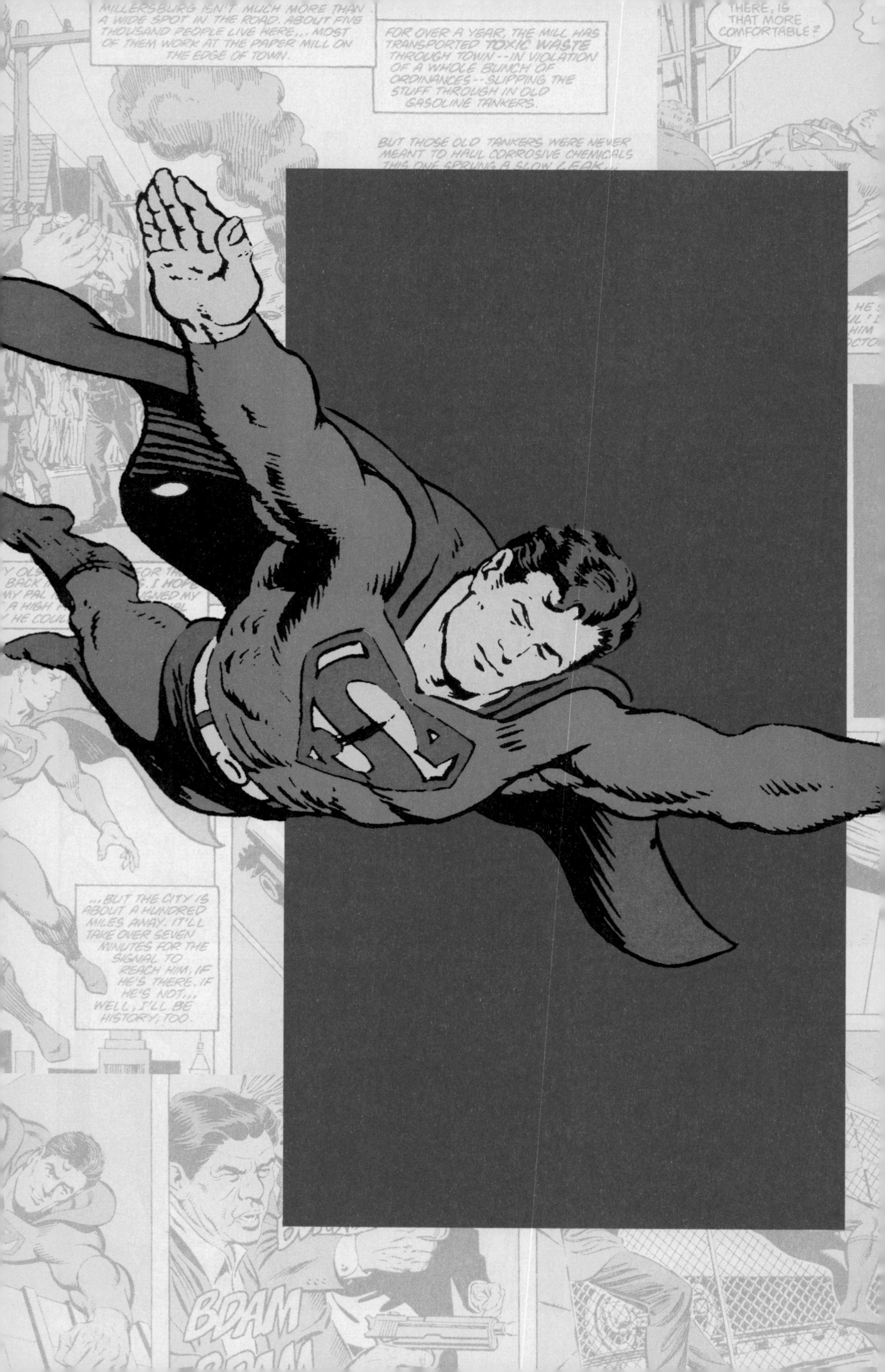
MILLERSBURG ISN'T MUCH MORE THAN A WIDE SPOT IN THE ROAD. ABOUT FIVE THOUSAND PEOPLE LIVE HERE... MOST OF THEM WORK AT THE PAPER MILL ON THE EDGE OF TOWN.
FOR OVER A YEAR, THE MILL HAS TRANSPORTED TOXIC WASTE THROUGH TOWN--IN VIOLATION OF A WHOLE BUNCH OF ORDINANCES--SLIPPING THE STUFF THROUGH IN OLD GASOLINE TANKERS.
BUT THOSE OLD TANKERS WERE NEVER MEANT TO HAUL CORROSIVE CHEMICALS
THERE, IS THAT MORE COMFORTABLE?
...BUT THE CITY IS ABOUT A HUNDRED MILES AWAY. IT'LL TAKE OVER SEVEN MINUTES FOR THE SIGNAL TO REACH HIM, IF HE'S THERE. IF HE'S NOT... WELL, I'LL BE HISTORY, TOO.
BDAM

Cover art by Kerry Gammill and Bob McLeod.

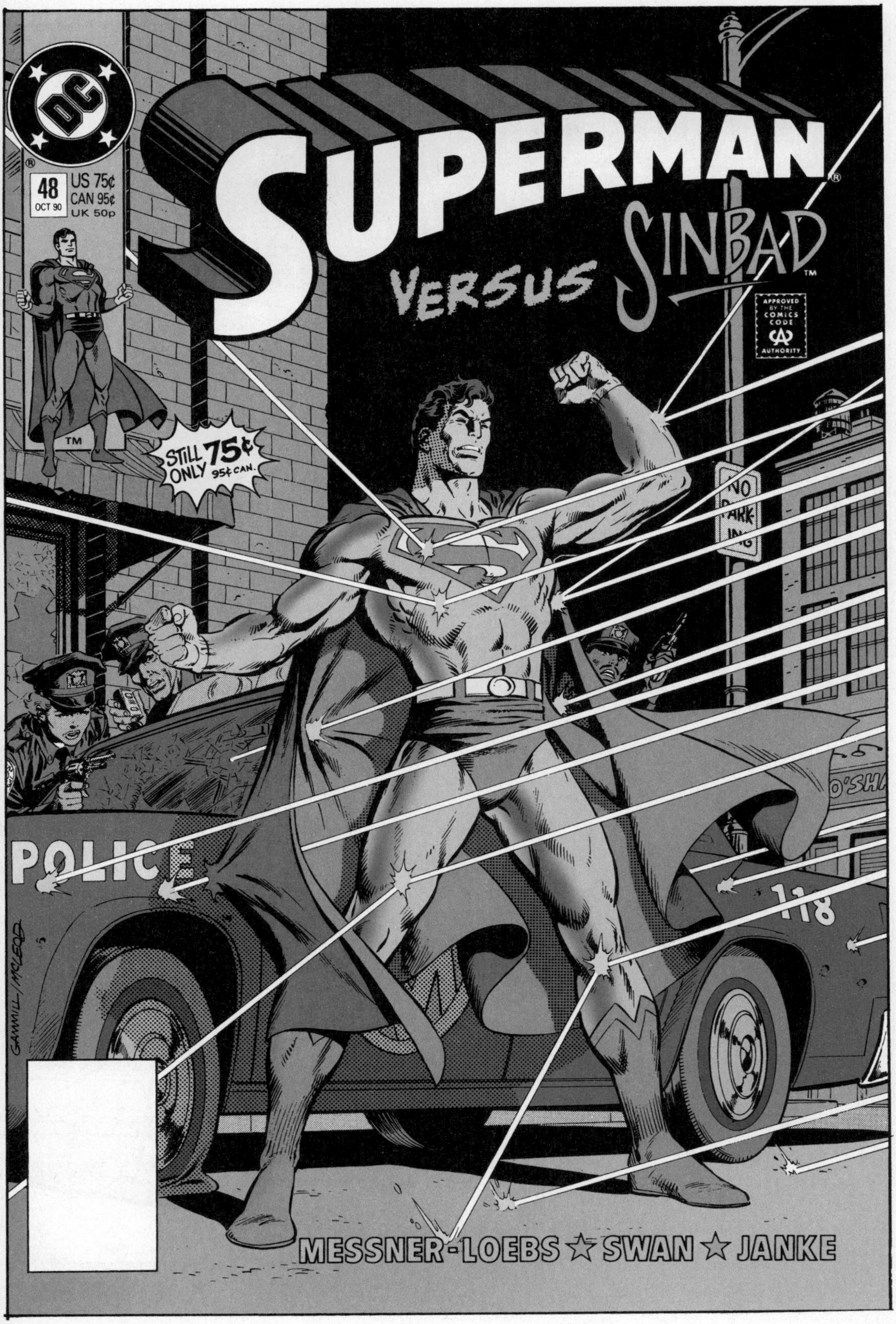

DC
SUPERMAN
48
OCT 90
US 75¢
CAN 95¢
UK 50p
TM
STILL ONLY 75¢ 95¢ CAN.
VERSUS SINBAD
APPROVED BY THE COMICS CODE AUTHORITY
NO PARKING
POLICE
118
O'SHA
GAMMILL/MCLEOD
MESSNER-LOEBS ☆ SWAN ☆ JANKE

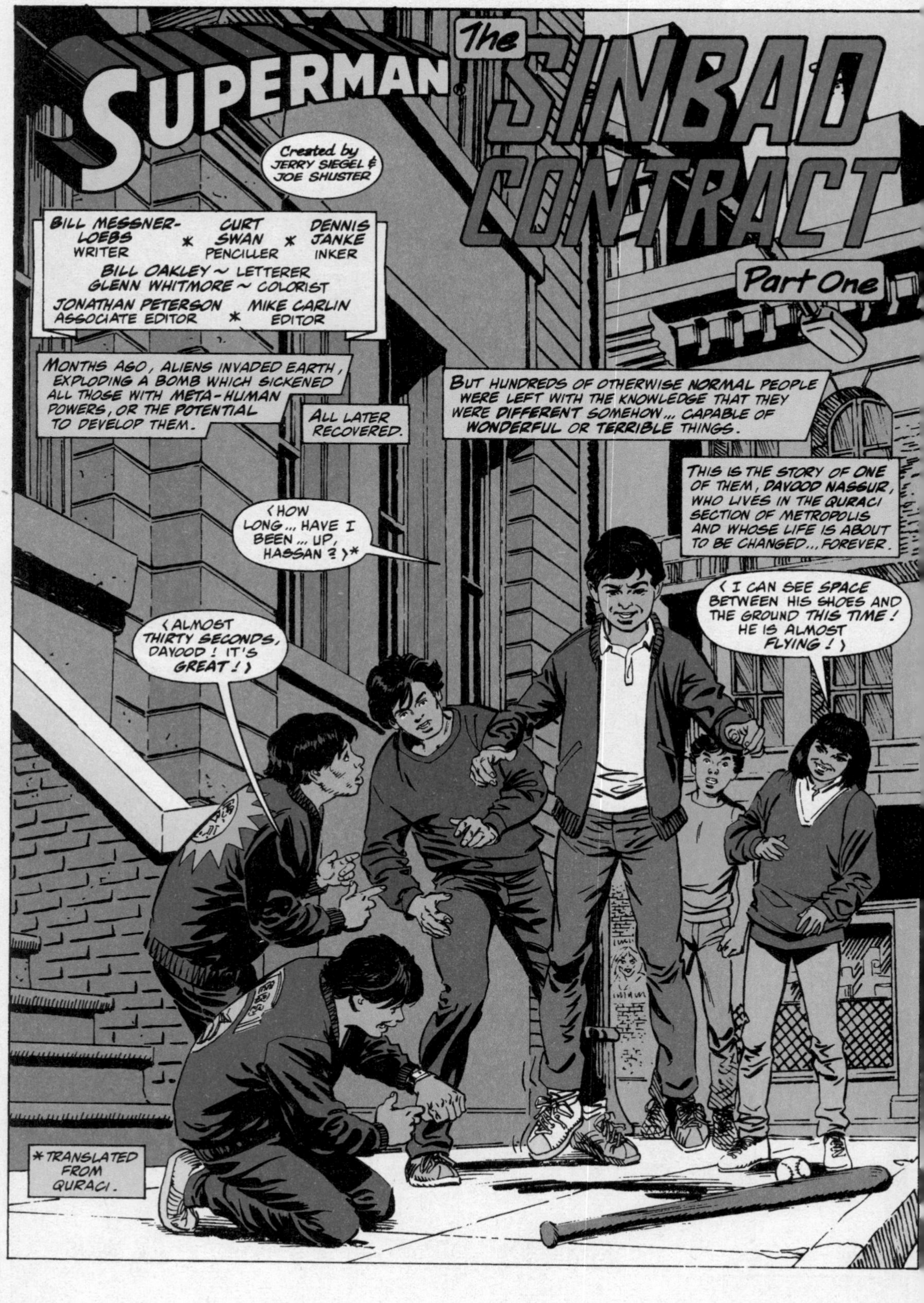
SUPERMAN
The SINBAD CONTRACT
Part One
Created by JERRY SIEGEL & JOE SHUSTER
BILL MESSNER-LOEBS WRITER * CURT SWAN PENCILLER * DENNIS JANKE INKER
BILL OAKLEY ~ LETTERER
GLENN WHITMORE ~ COLORIST
JONATHAN PETERSON ASSOCIATE EDITOR * MIKE CARLIN EDITOR
MONTHS AGO, ALIENS INVADED EARTH, EXPLODING A BOMB WHICH SICKENED ALL THOSE WITH META-HUMAN POWERS, OR THE POTENTIAL TO DEVELOP THEM.
ALL LATER RECOVERED.
BUT HUNDREDS OF OTHERWISE NORMAL PEOPLE WERE LEFT WITH THE KNOWLEDGE THAT THEY WERE DIFFERENT SOMEHOW... CAPABLE OF WONDERFUL OR TERRIBLE THINGS.
THIS IS THE STORY OF ONE OF THEM, DAVOOD NASSUR, WHO LIVES IN THE QURACI SECTION OF METROPOLIS AND WHOSE LIFE IS ABOUT TO BE CHANGED... FOREVER.
‹HOW LONG... HAVE I BEEN... UP, HASSAN?›*
‹ALMOST THIRTY SECONDS, DAVOOD! IT'S GREAT!›
‹I CAN SEE SPACE BETWEEN HIS SHOES AND THE GROUND THIS TIME! HE IS ALMOST FLYING!›
*TRANSLATED FROM QURACI.

⟨I DID IT! I KNEW I COULD!⟩

⟨YOU'VE BEEN TRYING EVER SINCE YOU GOT SICK! PRETTY SOON YOU'LL BE THE MOST POWERFUL GUY IN THE UNIVERSE!⟩

⟨I DON'T KNOW ABOUT THAT, BUT IF I CAN LIFT MYSELF, I SHOULD BE ABLE TO REPEL THINGS, TOO...⟩

⟨ISMAIL, GET THAT BALL AND THROW IT AT ME... HARD!⟩

⟨OKAY.⟩

THUNK

⟨OOHH... MAYBE NOT THAT HARD.⟩

⟨HERE, DAVOOD...! CATCH THIS!⟩

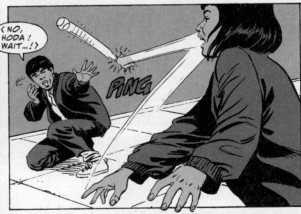

⟨NO, HODA! WAIT...!⟩

PING

⟨IT... IT WORKED.⟩

⟨DAVOOD! HASSAN! HODA! TIME FOR DINNER!⟩

A BUNCH OF KIDS GOING IN FOR SUPPER... IT'S GETTING TO BE THAT TIME...

MAYBE I'LL DROP IN AT THE *PLANET* AND SEE IF CAT OR JIMMY'S WORKING LATE.

WE COULD ALL GO OUT FOR MEATBALL AND MOZZARELLA SANDWICHES AT GEORGIO'S.

IT'S A QUIET NIGHT. I'LL JUST ZIG-ZAG ACROSS THE RIVER AND CALL IT A SUCCESSFUL *PATROL.*

I TELL YOU, GINGER, I SAW A GUY WITH A SHOTGUN SNEAKIN' AROUND THE BACK. THIS COULD BE A *MAJOR* CRACK HOUSE.

RIGHT, FRED. OR IT *COULD* BE A MAJOR *LAUNDROMAT,* LIKE THE LAST PLACE YOU INSISTED WE BUST.

IT WOULDN'T HAVE BEEN SO BAD, IF YOU HADN'T BEAT UP THE *NUN!*

I DIDN'T BEAT HER UP, I TACKLED HER... AND ONLY BECAUSE *YOU* SCREAMED OUT SHE HAD A *GUN!*

WELLLL... SHE SHOULDN'T BE CARRYING AROUND GUN-METAL WRAPPED FRENCH BREAD!

FRED, ONE OF THESE DAYS YOU'RE GONNA GET ME KILLED...

BLAM

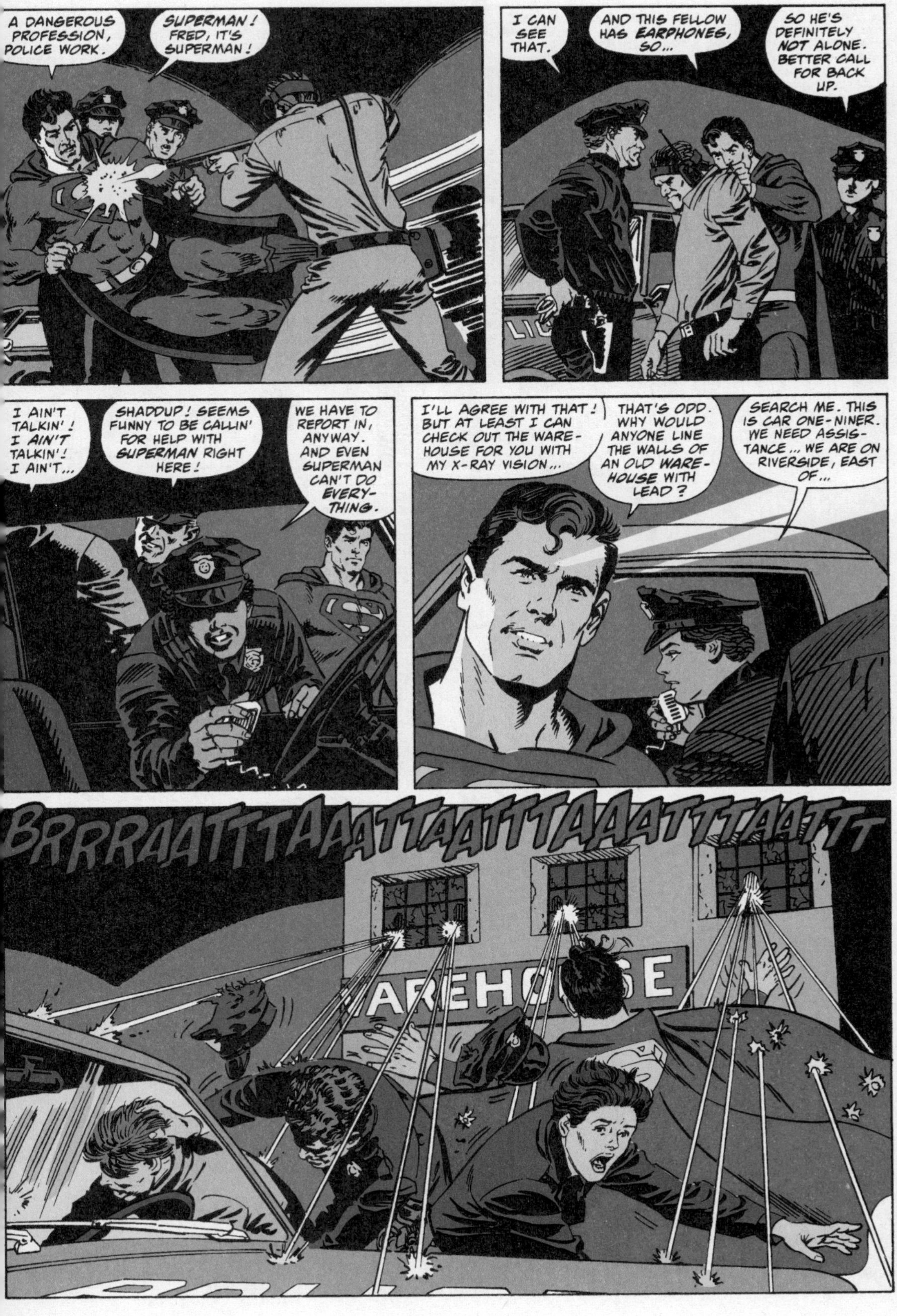
A DANGEROUS PROFESSION, POLICE WORK.
SUPERMAN! FRED, IT'S SUPERMAN!
I CAN SEE THAT.
AND THIS FELLOW HAS EARPHONES, SO...
SO HE'S DEFINITELY NOT ALONE. BETTER CALL FOR BACK UP.
I AIN'T TALKIN'! I AIN'T TALKIN'! I AIN'T...
SHADDUP! SEEMS FUNNY TO BE CALLIN' FOR HELP WITH SUPERMAN RIGHT HERE!
WE HAVE TO REPORT IN, ANYWAY. AND EVEN SUPERMAN CAN'T DO EVERYTHING.
I'LL AGREE WITH THAT! BUT AT LEAST I CAN CHECK OUT THE WAREHOUSE FOR YOU WITH MY X-RAY VISION...
THAT'S ODD. WHY WOULD ANYONE LINE THE WALLS OF AN OLD WAREHOUSE WITH LEAD?
SEARCH ME. THIS IS CAR ONE-NINER. WE NEED ASSISTANCE... WE ARE ON RIVERSIDE, EAST OF...
BRRRAATTTAAATTAATTTAAATTTAATTT

‹...AND I GOT ALMOST *THREE* INCHES OFF THE GROUND TODAY, MOM! IT WAS *GREAT!* AND I MADE A KIND OF *SHIELD* WHEN...›

‹ALL THIS TALK OF *POWER* WORRIES ME. YOU SHOULDN'T DRAW *ATTENTION* TO YOURSELF. IT'S DANGEROUS.›

‹NOT TO MENTION *STUPID!* WHAT *GOOD* DOES IT DO, FLOATING THREE INCHES UP?›

‹WELL...SOON I'LL BE ABLE TO REACH THE HIGH SHELVES WITHOUT A LADDER AND I CAN HELP UNCLE JAHIR RESHINGLE THE ROOF...!›

‹HUH! BETTER YOU SHOULD DROP FROM THE SKIES LIKE AN *AVENGER* AND PROTECT THIS NEIGHBORHOOD!›

‹YES, UNCLE JAHIR HAS BEEN HELD UP IN THE STORE *THREE* TIMES!›

‹RIGHT. THE *BARBARIANS* ARE AT THE GATES! THIS IS SO PARANOID...!›

‹THE POLICE DON'T *CARE!* THE *COSTUMES* DON'T CARE! NO ONE OUTSIDE GIVES A *DAMN* ABOUT US!›

‹WE HAVE TO BE STRONG! OTHERWISE, WE'LL BE DESTROYED!›

⟨SORAYA, YOU HAVE A SMART MOUTH! YOU DON'T KNOW WHAT YOUR FATHER AND I WENT THROUGH!⟩

⟨ALLAH, SAVE US! THIS WILL BE THE "HOW WE SUFFERED UNDER THE CRUEL SHAH" SPEECH!⟩

⟨YOU CHILDREN FORGET HOW WE ALL SUFFERED UNDER THE CRUEL SHAH!⟩

⟨ALL QURACI GROANED IN FEAR AND PAIN! IT WAS A NIGHTMARE!⟩

⟨YOUR FATHER DIED IN PRISON... I LOST MY HAND TO THE SUBTLE HUMOR OF THE SECRET POLICE. EIGHT YEARS AGO, WE FLED HERE.⟩

⟨NOW THAT THE SHAH IS OVERTHROWN, IT IS TOO LATE FOR ME TO RETURN. OUR LIVES ARE HERE. BUT YOU MUST NOT FORGET.⟩

⟨WE CAN'T FORGET! NO ONE LETS US!⟩

⟨AT SCHOOL, THEY SAY THE COLONEL IS AN EVIL MAN, WORSE THAN THE SHAH! AND THEY WHISPER "TER-RORIST, TERROR-IST" BEHIND OUR BACKS!⟩

⟨THAT'S WHY I LET THE KIDS CALL ME "DAVID" RATHER THAN "DAVOOD." IT'S EASIER.⟩

⟨YOU PRETEND YOU'RE NOT AN ARAB, NOT QURACI? THAT IS VERY BAD!⟩

⟨AWW, TO THEM, "ARAB" MEANS SINBAD THE SAILOR OR ALI BABA AND THE FORTY THIEVES! OR SOMEBODY WHO BLOWS UP AIR-PLANES!⟩

⟨IF THEY INSULT YOU, THEN YOU FIGHT! MAKE THEM RESPECT YOU!⟩

⟨JAHIR...DON'T BE MAD... IT DOES NO GOOD!⟩

‹ I KNOW, MUNEA. THEY THINK OF US AS IGNORANT *PEASANTS* WHO BELIEVE IN *GENII* AND *FLYING CARPETS*. BUT YOU KIDS WILL PROVE THEM *WRONG!* ›

‹ YOU WILL GO TO SCHOOL, GET *GOOD JOBS*, NOT WORK IN A GROCERY STORE YOUR WHOLE LIFE, LIKE ME... ›

‹ I DON'T *NEED* TO GO TO SCHOOL! NOT EVEN *SUPERMAN* C'N DO THIS! ›

‹ AND WHO'S GOING TO PAY YOU TO DO THAT? A *FREAK SHOW*? ›

‹ HERE. IF YOU HAVE SO MUCH ENERGY TO FIGHT, THEN YOU CAN *BOTH* CLEAN UP TONIGHT! ›

‹ IT'S BETTER THAN BEING A *STUPID* SECRETARY! ›

‹ YOU'RE JUST *JEALOUS!* LEXCORP'S A WONDERFUL PLACE TO WORK! AND THERE'S LOTS OF ROOM FOR *ADVANCEMENT!* ›

‹ WHAT...? ›

‹ BUT... BUT... ›

‹ THIS IS *YOUR* FAULT! ›

‹ WELL... LEXCORP IS A GOOD PLACE TO WORK. I THINK *EXCITING* THINGS WILL HAPPEN TO ME THERE... ›

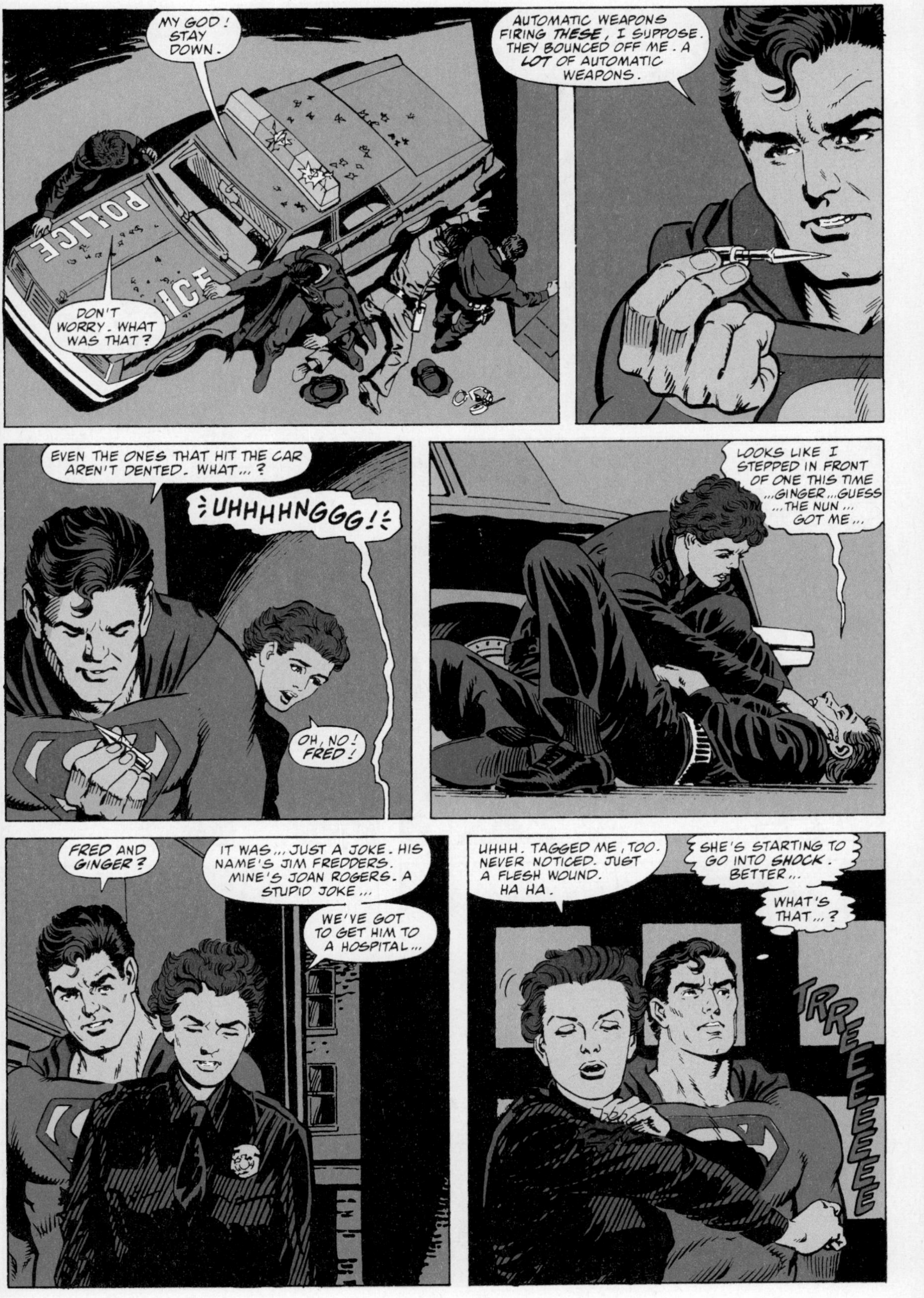
MY GOD! STAY DOWN.
POLICE
ICE
DON'T WORRY. WHAT WAS THAT?
AUTOMATIC WEAPONS FIRING THESE, I SUPPOSE. THEY BOUNCED OFF ME. A LOT OF AUTOMATIC WEAPONS.
EVEN THE ONES THAT HIT THE CAR AREN'T DENTED. WHAT...?
UHHHHNGGG!
OH, NO! FRED!
LOOKS LIKE I STEPPED IN FRONT OF ONE THIS TIME ...GINGER...GUESS ...THE NUN... GOT ME...
FRED AND GINGER?
IT WAS... JUST A JOKE. HIS NAME'S JIM FREDDERS. MINE'S JOAN ROGERS. A STUPID JOKE...
WE'VE GOT TO GET HIM TO A HOSPITAL...
UHHH. TAGGED ME, TOO. NEVER NOTICED. JUST A FLESH WOUND. HA HA.
SHE'S STARTING TO GO INTO SHOCK. BETTER...
WHAT'S THAT...?
TRREEEEEEEE

SSSSSSSSSSS

LOOK OUT!

A LASER BEAM? WHAT *IS* THIS?

THEY'RE COMING FROM THE *WAREHOUSE!* HOLD IT, FLYBOYS! YOU'RE UNDER *ARREST!*

BLAM BLAM

TOOOOSH

BLAM BLAM BLAM

WHUDD

I FELT THAT... WHAT KIND OF WEAPONS ARE THESE?!

SUPERMAN! OVER THERE!

MY...GOD.

GONE...FASTER THAN I CAN FOLLOW.

WHAT... WAS IT?

I HAVE... NO IDEA.

THE SEAT FROM THE PATROL CAR WILL MAKE A GOOD STRETCHER UNTIL WE REACH THE HOSPITAL.

COME ON. WE'VE GOT TO SEE IF THEY LEFT ANYTHING.

WHAT IN GOD'S NAME HAVE I BLUNDERED INTO?

"WE HAVE RECEIVED YOUR SHIPMENT OF 5900 UNITS FOR *OPERATION NIGHTMARE*. HOWEVER, SEVERAL OF THE UNITS ..."

‹ IT IS SO EXCITING, WORKING ON LEXCORP'S PHILAN-THROPIES ... I WON-DER WHAT ALL THESE CODENAMES REALLY MEAN ...? ›

HELLO, MR. LUTHOR.

HELLO, MR. LUTHOR.

HELLO, MR. LUTHOR.

HELLO, MR. LUTHOR.

HELLO, MR. LUTHOR.

HELLO, MR. LUTHOR.

HELLO, MR. LUTHOR.

HELLO, MR. LUTHOR.

HELLO, MR. LUTHOR.

HELLO, MR. LUTHOR.

"...MALFUNCTIONED, CAUSING A DELAY..."

‹ IT'S LEX LUTHOR! ›

HELLO, MR. ...

MS. KREEL, ANY WORD FROM OUR COURIER ON THE, UM ... *BLACK BELT* MATTER?

NO, SIR. HE MUST'VE BEEN ... DETAINED.

PITY. I NEED NEW FILES ON ALL THESE COM-PANIES. THE INFORMATION SHOULD BE UPDATED.AND NEW QUERY LETTERS SENT ... *BEFORE* THE WEEKEND.

YES, SIR.

MS. NASSUR WILL BE *GLAD* TO STAY LATE TONIGHT.

UH ... YES, MA'AM.

LAST NIGHT WAS ONE OF THE *WEIRDEST* NIGHTS OF MY LIFE. EVERYTHING HAPPENED SO *QUICKLY,* I...

'MORNING, KENT. YOU HEAR ABOUT THE *TERRORISTS* DOWN BY THE RIVER?

UH, SOMETHING. A COUPLE OF POLICE WERE SHOT, RIGHT?

RIGHT. AND THEN *SUPERMAN* SHOWED UP AND RAN THE *TOWEL-HEADS* OFF.

UH... I DIDN'T READ ANYWHERE THAT IT WAS *ARABS,* KEITH.

ISN'T IT *ALWAYS?*

LET ME TELL YOU, KENT... WE'D BE A LOT *SAFER* IF SUPERMAN WAS GIVEN *TOTAL POWER!*

HE NEVER GETS TIRED, RIGHT? WELL, HE COULD JUST *CIRCLE* THE GLOBE WITH HIS *X-RAYS* ON AND SEE *EVERYTHING!*

AND ANYBODY WHO WAS OUT OF LINE... HE'D JUST *SWAT* 'EM!

I DON'T THINK I'D WANT ANYONE TO HAVE *THAT* MUCH POWER. I'M AFRAID HE'D BE TEMPTED TO *MISUSE* IT.

HE DOES MAKE *MISTAKES,* YOU KNOW.

AHH, YOU KNOW WHAT YOUR *PROBLEM* IS, KENT?

YOU DON'T HAVE THE SAME *FAITH* IN SUPERMAN THAT THE REST OF US DO!

MUCH LATER THAT EVENING...

⟨OHHH, I HATE THIS! I'M SO TIRED... GOOD THING I CALLED MUTI* AND TOLD HER I'D BE LATE.⟩

*MUTI : MOTHER.

⟨THAT'S IT. I'VE *GOT* TO GET SOME FRESH AIR. MAYBE THE SIDE DOOR TO THE PARKING LOT IS STILL OPEN.⟩

⟨THIS IS BETTER JUST BECAUSE I'M THE *NEW KID*, MS. KREEL DUMPS EVERYTHING OFF ON ME. MAYBE UNCLE JAHIR IS RIGHT. MAYBE...⟩

⟨HEY, SIS!⟩

⟨DAVOOD! WHAT ARE YOU DOING HERE?⟩

⟨I BROUGHT YOU A SANDWICH AND SOME HOT COFFEE. JUST TO WIN YOUR *ETERNAL GRATITUDE!*⟩

⟨CLOWN! THANK YOU!⟩

⟨YOU WANT A LIFT HOME? IT'S LATE.⟩

⟨I CAN'T. I'LL PROBABLY BE HERE ALL NIGHT. I...⟩

HELP ME... I ESCAPED FROM THEM...

HERE... ⟨COF-COF⟩... TAKE THIS... DON'T LET *THEM* GET IT...⟨COFF⟩

YOU... YOU'RE HURT!

TELL *LUTHOR*... TELL HIM... MY DEBT IS... ⟨COFF-COFF⟩ PAID... HE CAN'T REACH ME... ANYMOOORRR⟨⟩

102

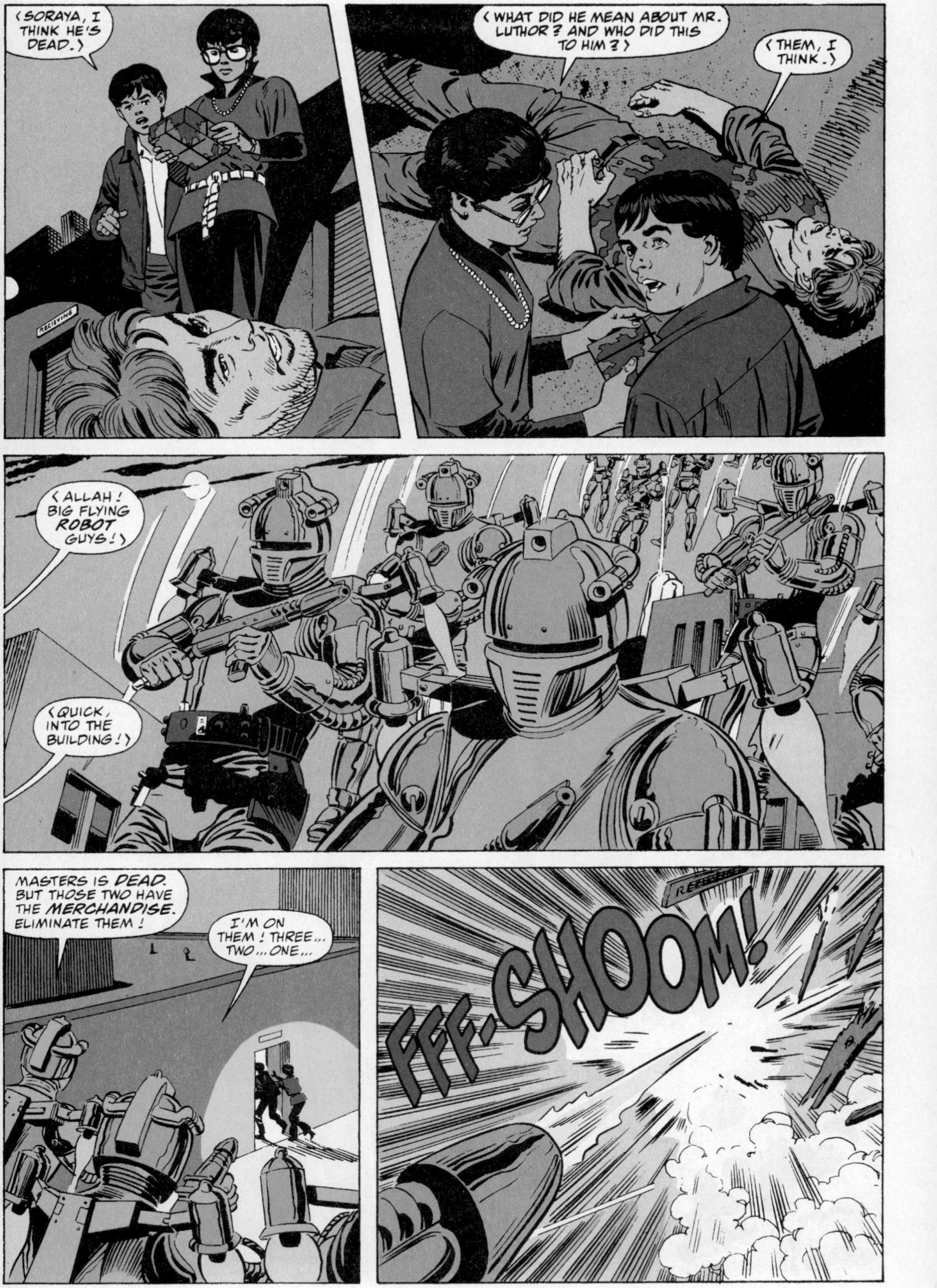
‹SORAYA, I THINK HE'S DEAD.›
‹WHAT DID HE MEAN ABOUT MR. LUTHOR? AND WHO DID THIS TO HIM?›
‹THEM, I THINK.›
‹ALLAH! BIG FLYING ROBOT GUYS!›
‹QUICK, INTO THE BUILDING!›
MASTERS IS DEAD. BUT THOSE TWO HAVE THE MERCHANDISE. ELIMINATE THEM!
I'M ON THEM! THREE... TWO...ONE...
FFF-SHOOM!

IT SOUNDED LIKE AN EXPLOSION COMING FROM *LEXCORP*. WHAT *NOW*?

WHOA. WHAT WAS *THAT*?

I'D BETTER CHECK THIS OUT... SOMETHING COULD BE SERIOUSLY...

...WRONG. THEY WEREN'T CAUGHT IN THE SHOCK-WAVE. SPREAD OUT QUICKLY AND...

"...SHOOT THEM ON SIGHT!"

⟨THEY... ⁊GASP⁊ ...BLEW IT UP! THEY JUST *BLEW AWAY* THE WHOLE... ⁊PANT⁊ ...SIDE OF THE BUILDING!⟩

⟨KEEP GOING! IF THEY CAN'T *FIND* US, THEY CAN'T BLOW US AWAY!⟩

⟨I'VE GOT TO STOP. I THINK WE'VE LOST THEM.⟩

⟨WELL, FOR A MINUTE. WE'VE GOT TO FIND A PHONE.⟩

⟨LET'S OPEN THE PACKAGE!⟩

⟨WHAT?⟩

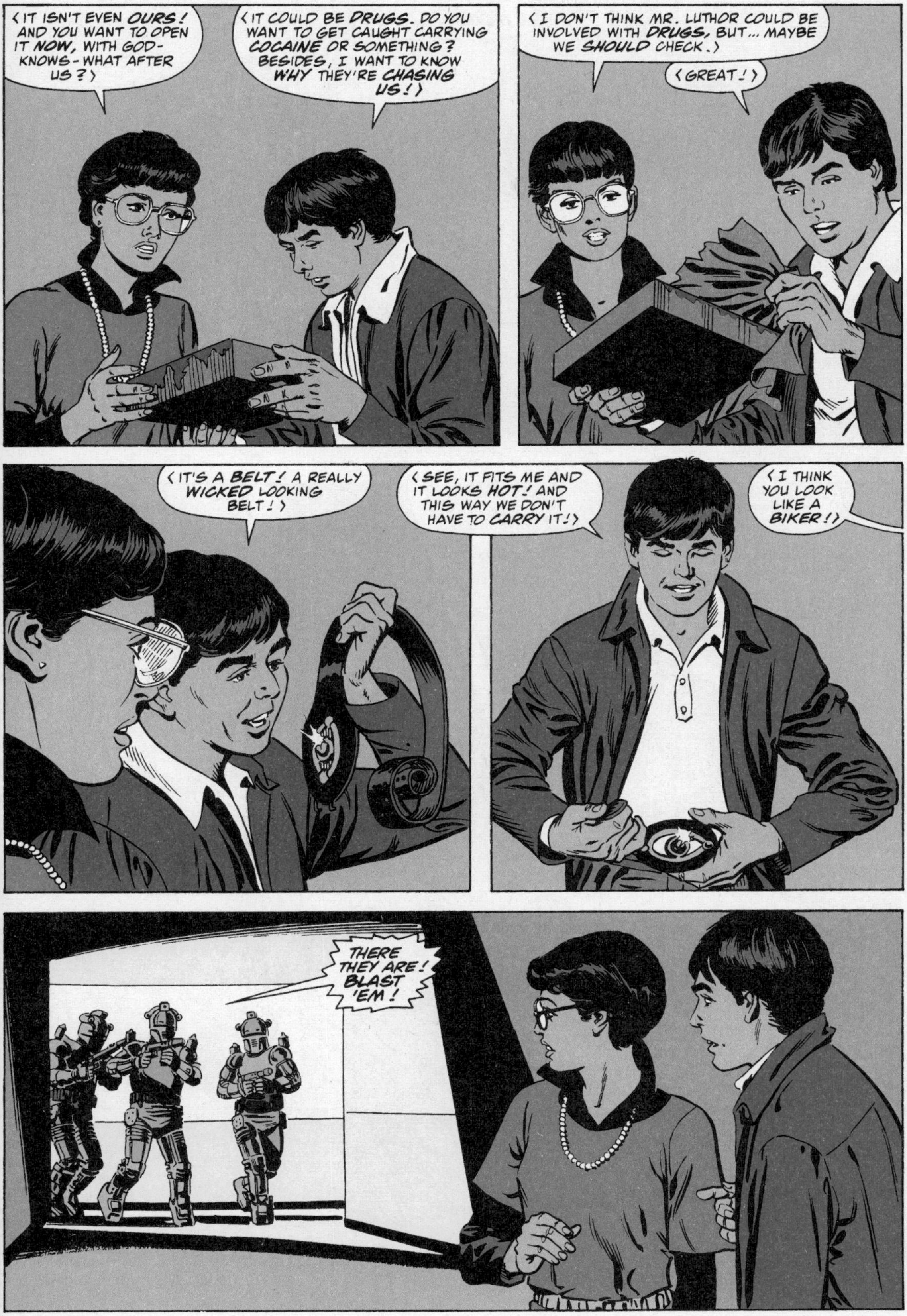

‹IT ISN'T EVEN OURS! AND YOU WANT TO OPEN IT NOW, WITH GOD-KNOWS-WHAT AFTER US?›
‹IT COULD BE DRUGS. DO YOU WANT TO GET CAUGHT CARRYING COCAINE OR SOMETHING? BESIDES, I WANT TO KNOW WHY THEY'RE CHASING US!›
‹I DON'T THINK MR. LUTHOR COULD BE INVOLVED WITH DRUGS, BUT... MAYBE WE SHOULD CHECK.›
‹GREAT!›
‹IT'S A BELT! A REALLY WICKED LOOKING BELT!›
‹SEE, IT FITS ME AND IT LOOKS HOT! AND THIS WAY WE DON'T HAVE TO CARRY IT!›
‹I THINK YOU LOOK LIKE A BIKER!›
THERE THEY ARE! BLAST 'EM!

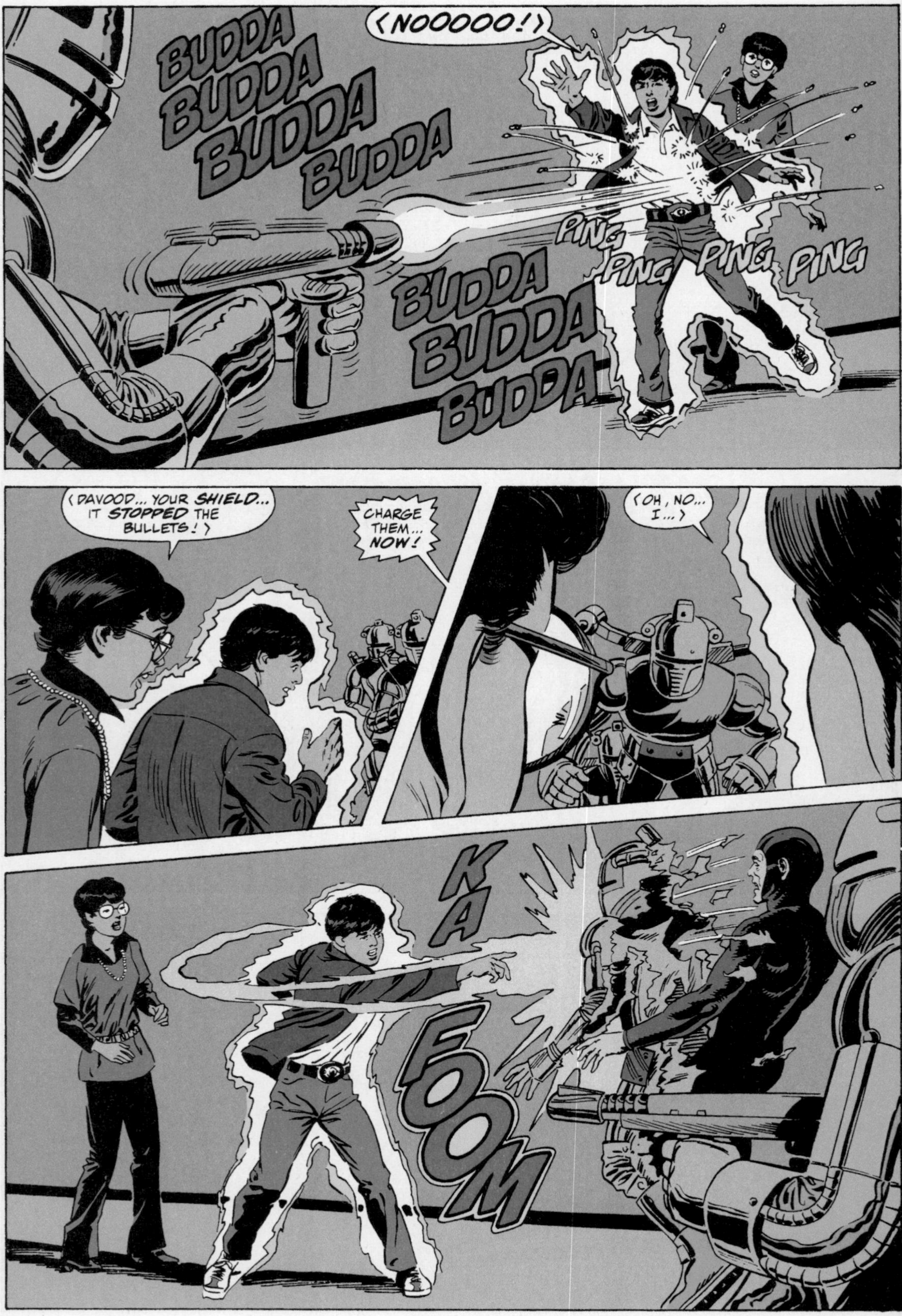

BUDDA BUDDA BUDDA BUDDA
⟨NOOOOO!⟩
BUDDA BUDDA BUDDA
PING PING PING PING
⟨DAVOOD... YOUR SHIELD... IT STOPPED THE BULLETS!⟩
CHARGE THEM... NOW!
⟨OH, NO... I...⟩
KA
FOOM

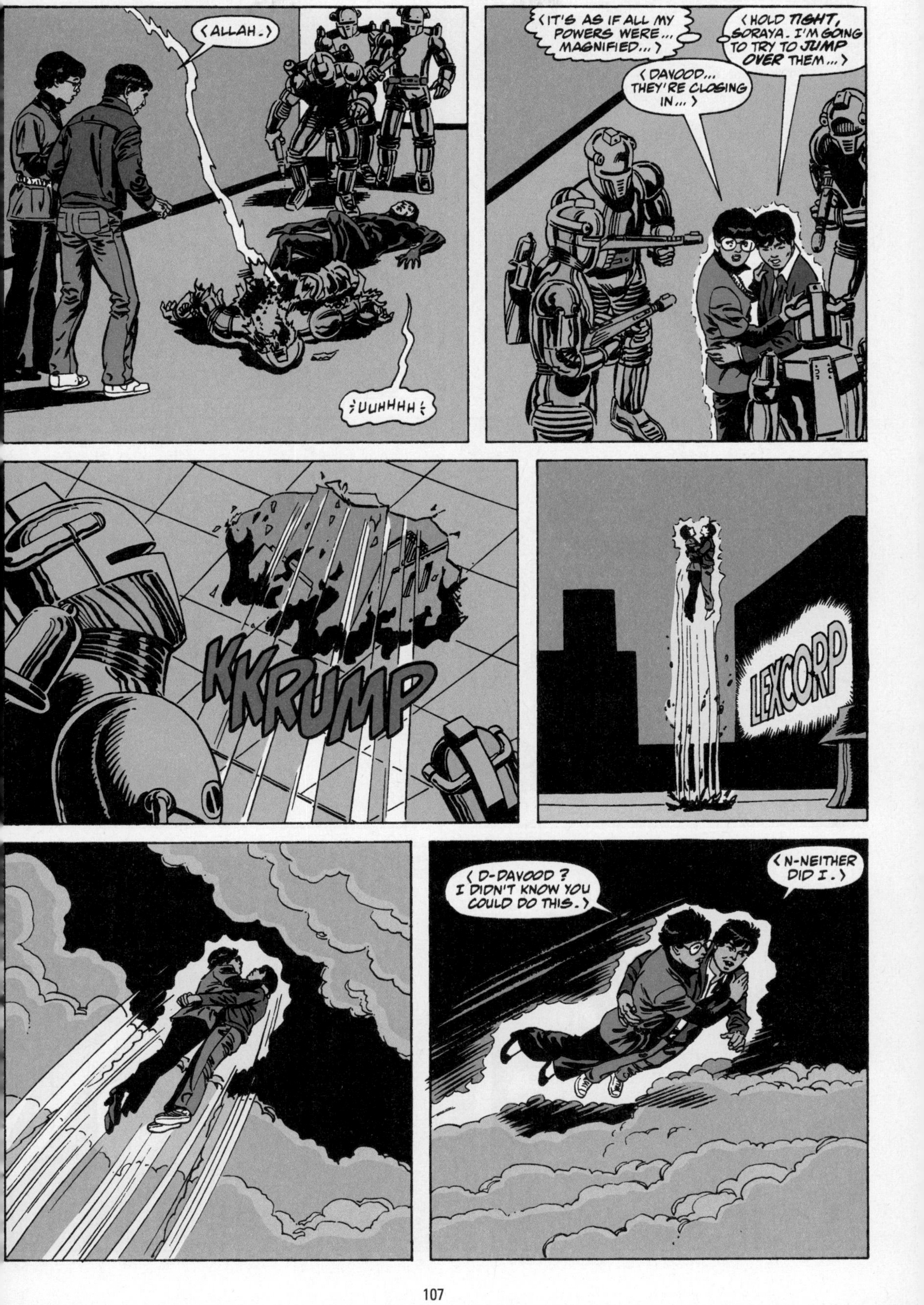
‹ALLAH.›
¦UUHHHH¦
‹IT'S AS IF ALL MY POWERS WERE... MAGNIFIED...›
‹HOLD TIGHT, SORAYA. I'M GOING TO TRY TO JUMP OVER THEM...›
‹DAVOOD... THEY'RE CLOSING IN...›
KKRUMP
LEXCORP
‹D-DAVOOD? I DIDN'T KNOW YOU COULD DO THIS.›
‹N-NEITHER DID I.›

< MAYBE WE SHOULD JUST *FLOAT* AWAY AND LEAVE THEM DOWN THERE. >

< WE *CAN'T!* UNCLE JAHIR'S TRUCK IS DOWN THERE! >

< WELL, THEN WE COULD--! HERE THEY COME AGAIN! >

BRATATATA TATATATATAT

< KEEP YOUR HEAD DOWN, SORAYA! >

< THEY'RE *RUNNING,* DAVOOD! LET'S GET OUT OF HERE! >

< MAYBE WE'VE SCARED THEM OFF. >

MAYBE NOT. HEH-HEH...

"HEH-HEH" YOURSELF!

SCRUNCH

SUPERMAN! ...UH ...THE ROCKETPACK. IT'S RIGGED TO...

FOOOOOM!

WHAT... IS GOING ON HERE?

<WHAT WAS THAT? A LIGHTNING BOLT?>

<NO! IT'S SUPERMAN!>

<WE'VE GOT TO GET OUT OF HERE! HE'LL NEVER LISTEN TO OUR SIDE OF THIS!>

<RIGHT! REMEMBER HOW HE TRASHED QURACI LAST YEAR? IF HE FINDS OUT WE'RE QURACI, HE'LL TEAR US APART!>

<WE'RE SAFE. THEY'VE ALL LEFT.>

<THAT SOUNDS LIKE A REALLY GOOD IDEA FOR US, TOO! GET TO THE TRUCK! HURRY!>

LEXCO

HOLD IT A SECOND, YOUNG LADY! THERE'RE A COUPLE OF QUESTIONS I NEED ANSWERED!

<DAVOOD!>

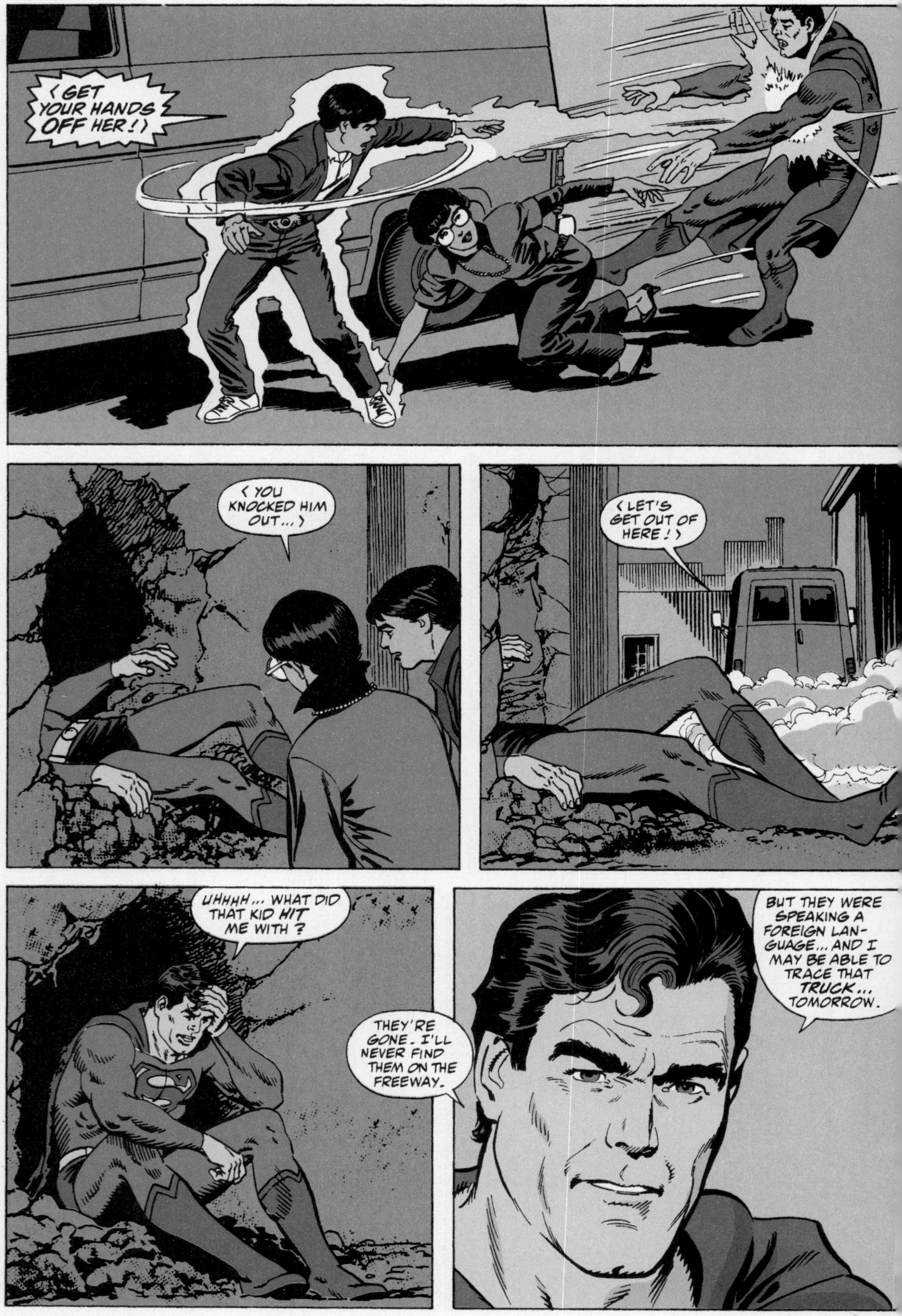
‹ GET YOUR HANDS OFF HER ! ›
‹ YOU KNOCKED HIM OUT... ›
‹ LET'S GET OUT OF HERE ! ›
UHHHH... WHAT DID THAT KID HIT ME WITH ?
THEY'RE GONE. I'LL NEVER FIND THEM ON THE FREEWAY.
BUT THEY WERE SPEAKING A FOREIGN LAN-GUAGE... AND I MAY BE ABLE TO TRACE THAT TRUCK... TOMORROW.

ELSEWHERE...

SO, THIS IS THE WAY IT ENDS.

I'M *RICH*, RICH BEYOND MOST MEN'S IMAGININGS... *ENTOMBED* WITH POWER...

AND YET, I CAN'T SAVE MYSELF. I'LL BE *DEAD* IN A YEAR.

AND I COULDN'T SAVE JERRY.

THE *WEAK-NESS* IS *WORSE*...

THE DOCTORS LOOK AT ME WITH *PITY* IN THEIR EYES... *ME!*

I'LL DIE AND MY EMPIRE WILL *CRUMBLE*. I'LL BE FORGOTTEN.

BUT IF I MUST *DIE*, IT WON'T BE AS THE *SECOND* MOST POWERFUL MAN ON EARTH...

SUPERMAN *MUST DIE FIRST!*

NEXT WEEK:
IN *ADVENTURES OF SUPERMAN* #471:

"SINBAD STRIKES AGAIN!"

★ ★ ★ ★ ★

IN TWO WEEKS:
IN *ACTION COMICS* #658:

"SINBAD'S SACRIFICE!"

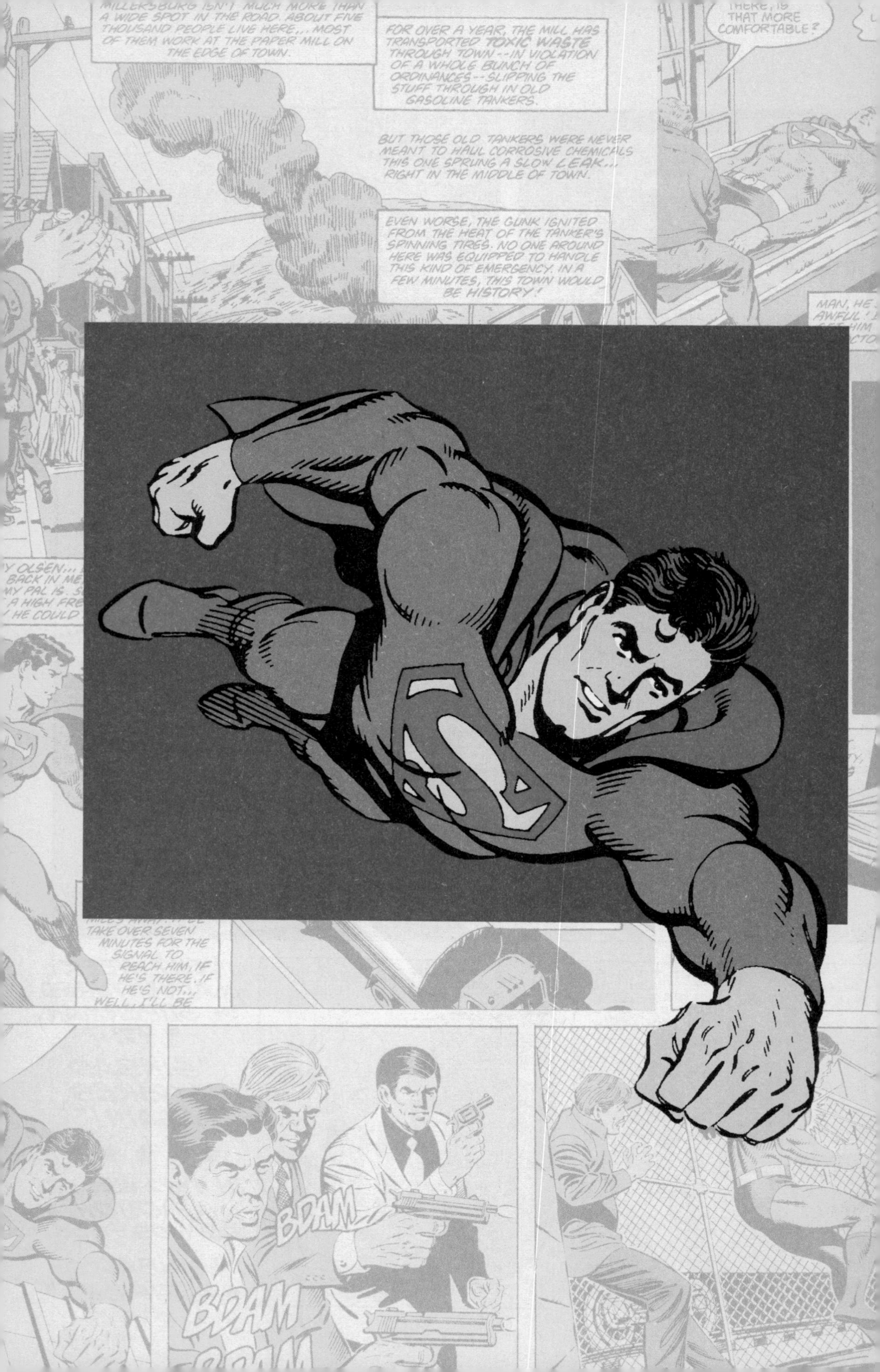

A WIDE SPOT IN THE ROAD. ABOUT FIVE THOUSAND PEOPLE LIVE HERE... MOST OF THEM WORK AT THE PAPER MILL ON THE EDGE OF TOWN.
FOR OVER A YEAR, THE MILL HAS TRANSPORTED TOXIC WASTE THROUGH TOWN--IN VIOLATION OF A WHOLE BUNCH OF ORDINANCES--SLIPPING THE STUFF THROUGH IN OLD GASOLINE TANKERS.
BUT THOSE OLD TANKERS WERE NEVER MEANT TO HAUL CORROSIVE CHEMICALS. THIS ONE SPRUNG A SLOW LEAK... RIGHT IN THE MIDDLE OF TOWN.
EVEN WORSE, THE GUNK IGNITED FROM THE HEAT OF THE TANKER'S SPINNING TIRES. NO ONE AROUND HERE WAS EQUIPPED TO HANDLE THIS KIND OF EMERGENCY. IN A FEW MINUTES, THIS TOWN WOULD BE HISTORY!
THAT MORE COMFORTABLE?
TAKE OVER SEVEN MINUTES FOR THE SIGNAL TO REACH HIM, IF HE'S THERE. IF HE'S NOT... WELL, I'LL BE
BDAM
BDAM

Cover art by Kerry Gammill and Bob McLeod.

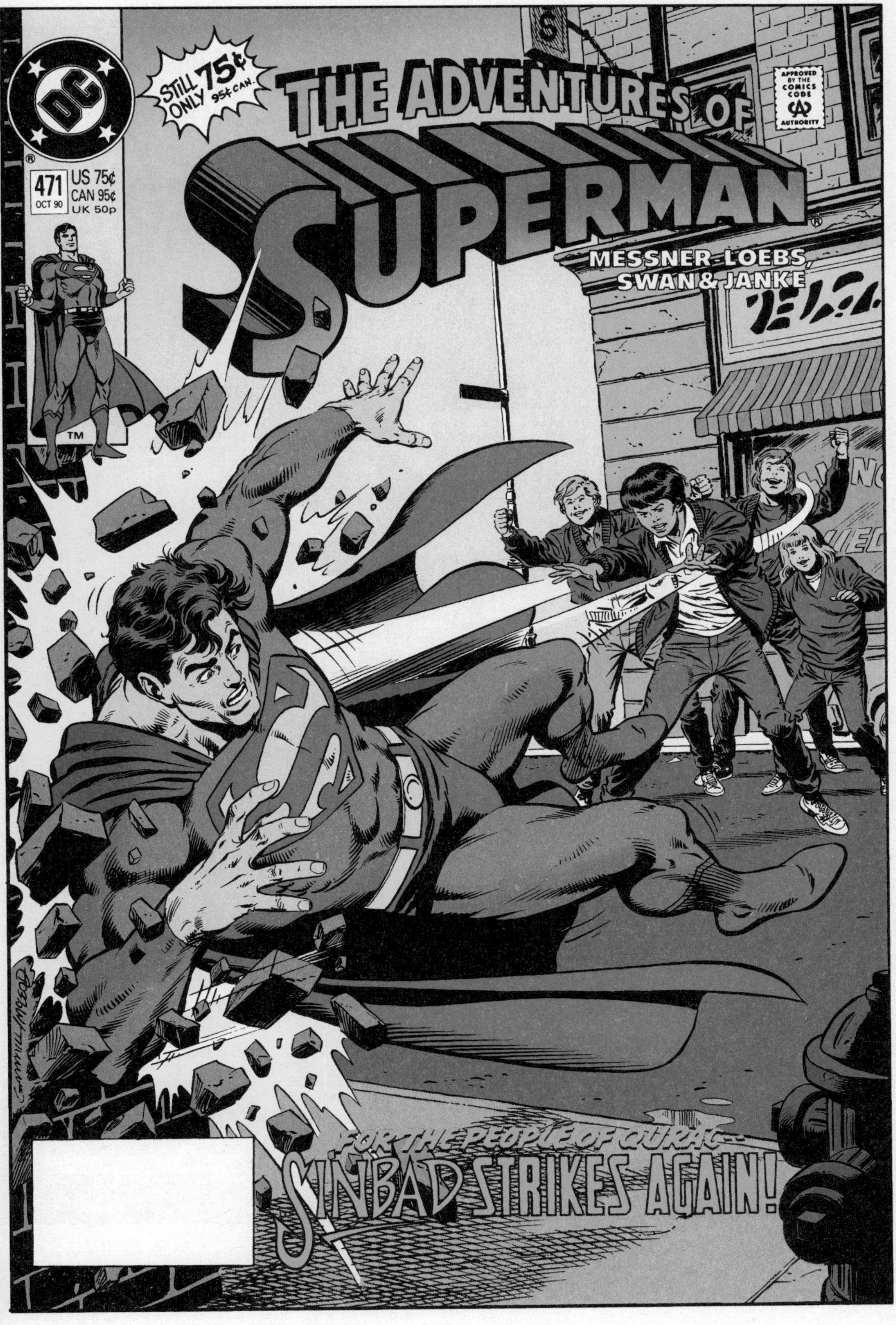

STILL ONLY 75¢ 95¢ CAN.
THE ADVENTURES OF
SUPERMAN
471 OCT 90
US 75¢ CAN 95¢ UK 50p
APPROVED BY THE COMICS CODE AUTHORITY
MESSNER-LOEBS, SWAN & JANKE
FOR THE PEOPLE OF QURAC--
SINBAD STRIKES AGAIN!

DEEP IN THE LITTLE QURAC SECTION OF METROPOLIS, WHILE MOST SLEEP, ONE SMALL GROUP KEEPS A WORRIED VIGIL. FOR DAVOOD NASSUR AND HIS FAMILY, LIFE WILL NEVER BE THE SAME.

The SINBAD CONTRACT
Part Two

BECAUSE EARLIER TODAY, DAVOOD NASSUR BECAME MORE THAN HUMAN.

‹AND THESE ARMORED MEN? YOU BEAT THEM ALL?›

‹AND I FLEW! LIKE A JET! IT WAS GREAT!›

NASSUR GROCERIES

QURAC

ONE WAY

SUPERMAN

Created by
JERRY SIEGEL &
JOE SHUSTER

BILL MESSNER-LOEBS   *   CURT SWAN   *   DENNIS JANKE
WRITER   PENCILLER   INKER
BILL OAKLEY ~ LETTERER
GLENN WHITMORE ~ COLORIST
JONATHAN PETERSON   *   MIKE CARLIN
ASSOCIATE EDITOR   EDITOR

‹...SO WE TOOK ABOUT AN HOUR GETTING HOME, MAKING SURE WE WEREN'T FOLLOWED.›

‹THIS IS ALL.... INCREDIBLE.›

‹APPARENTLY THE **BELT** AMPLIFIES THE POWERS I ALREADY HAD. WHEN I TAKE IT OFF, **NOTHING.**›

‹IT DOESN'T FEEL **WEIRD,** JUST COLD.›

‹IT MAKES ME NERVOUS.›

‹IT ISN'T YOURS. YOU MUST GIVE IT BACK TO MR. LUTHOR, OR WHOEVER IT REALLY BELONGS TO.›

‹YOUR MOTHER'S RIGHT! HAVING IT HERE WILL ONLY BRING DANGER TO THE WHOLE FAMILY!›

‹I'M NOT SURE WHO IT REALLY BELONGS TO. OR HOW TO GET IN TOUCH WITH THEM.›

‹THE... MAN THIS EVENING... HE WAS TALKING AS IF MR. LUTHOR WAS A **CRIMINAL** OF SOME KIND. AND THAT **CAN'T** BE RIGHT.›

‹YOU COULD BE A **HERO!** YOU CAN FIGHT **CRIMINALS** AND **MAD SCIENTISTS!**›

‹YOU COULD BE **SINBAD** AND FIGHT **MONSTERS!**›

‹ IT SURE FELT *GREAT* TO FLY... AND TO HAVE ALL THAT STRENGTH ! I EVEN TOOK OUT *SUPERMAN* ! ›

‹ TRUE. AND WHAT HAPPENS WHEN HE COMES LOOKING FOR YOU ? HE'LL RIP THIS WHOLE NEIGHBORHOOD APART TO FIND YOU ! ›

‹ AND WHAT ABOUT THOSE *OTHERS* ? THE ARMORED MEN ? WHAT CAN WE DO IF THEY...? ›

CRASH

‹ WHAT WAS THAT ? ›

‹ IT CAME FROM DOWNSTAIRS ! ›

‹ BURGLARS, PERHAPS... OR ONLY THE CAT... ›

‹ I'M GOING DOWN TO CHECK . ›

‹ NO, IT'S TOO DANGEROUS ! ›

‹ LET HIM GO, MUNEA ! FOR ONCE HE'S NOT ACTING LIKE A DREAMER OR A CHILD... ›

THUNK CRAASH!

116

HEY, JERRY, QUIT KNOCKIN' THINGS OVER, WILLYA? PEOPLE ARE GONNA GET DOWN HERE BEFORE WE FIND THE REGISTER!

COOL IT, TIMBO. IT DON'T MATTER HOW MUCH RACKET WE MAKE.

I KNOCKED OVER THIS PLACE BEFORE! THERE'S JUST ONE CRIPPLED GUY UPSTAIRS, HIS SISTER AND A BUNCH OF KIDS! THEY'RE ALL HIDING!

AND SO WHAT IF THEY CALL THE COPS? THE COPS DON'T LIKE TO COME TO THIS NEIGHBORHOOD!

MACK! SLICER! YOU GUYS FIND ANYTHING YET?

HEY, GUYS... DON'T MESS AROUND ON US NOW... WE GOTTA GET...

THUNK WHUMP!

UHHHHH...

YOU FEEBS JUST BOUGHT YOURSELVES A LOT OF TROUBLE.

FRESH VEGETABLES DELI MEAT and DAIRY

SCCRRAAASSSHHHT

MR. LUTHOR! MR. LUTHOR! WAKE UP! THERE'S BEEN AN ACCIDENT...

HUUMMM? THASS GOOD... DO THA...SOME...

GOODWIN? WHAT IS THIS? AN ACCIDENT? WHERE?

LEXCORP HEADQUARTERS. THEY'VE BEEN TRASHED!

THERE'S A HOLE THE SIZE OF A SMALL VAN DRILLED FROM THE MAIN FLOOR TO THE ROOF.

COULD IT HAVE BEEN A BOMB?

NEGATIVE. THE SIDE DOORS HAVE ALSO BEEN BLOWN AWAY. AND CARL MASTERS WAS FOUND, DEAD, BY THE PARKING LOT.

ALSO, WE FOUND TRACES OF ARMORED FIGHTING SUITS.

IT LOOKS LIKE MASTERS TRIED TO DELIVER THE BLACK BELT, BUT THE OPPOSITION FOUND HIM FIRST.

HOWEVER, FROM THE DAMAGE, IT LOOKS LIKE A THIRD PARTY WAS ALSO INVOLVED... POSSIBLY META-HUMAN.

AND THE BELT?

GONE.

DISPOSE OF THE BODY AND CLEAN UP AS MUCH OF THE DAMAGE AS POSSIBLE BEFORE MORNING.

THESE EVENTS NEVER HAPPENED.

AND, GOODWIN, FIND THAT BELT! ELIM- INATE WHOEVER STANDS IN YOUR WAY! BUT FIND THAT BELT!

NOW!!

I SAID NOW! GO!

¦AARRRRRGGG...!¦

THE PAIN! GOT TO FIGHT THE PAIN... FIGHT IT...

HAVE TO SIT... IF I CAN JUST SIT...

BETTER... BUT EACH BOUT WITH THE PAIN LEAVES ME A LITTLE WEAKER...

AND I CAN'T BE WEAK NOW...

NOT NOW...

IF I'M *EVER* GOING TO FIGURE OUT THE WEIRDNESS THAT HAPPENED YESTERDAY, I HAVE TO START HERE... AT METROPOLIS GENERAL HOSPITAL

SOMEHOW, EVERYONE SEEMS TO END UP HERE SOONER OR LATER ...HEROES, VILLAINS...

...VICTIMS. I HOPE THEY REMEMBER SOMETHING ABOUT THE ATTACK YESTERDAY.

OH, SORRY. I MUST'VE DOZED. WHO...?

PLEASE, GET YOUR REST. I'M A REPORTER ... CLARK KENT, FROM THE PLANET.

I'D LIKE TO TALK TO YOU ABOUT THE INCIDENT YESTERDAY.

I CAN'T TELL YOU MUCH. IT WAS A NIGHTMARE. FRED AND I WOULD'VE DIED IF *SUPERMAN* HADN'T BEEN THERE.

MAYBE. BUT SUPERMAN WAS NEVER IN ANY *REAL* DANGER. YOU TWO WERE RISKING YOUR *LIVES.*

I'D LIKE TO DO THE STORY FROM THAT PERSPECTIVE.

ALL EVERYBODY'S WANTED TO KNOW SINCE YESTERDAY IS "WHAT DID *SUPERMAN DO?* WHAT'S HE *LIKE?* "

YOU'RE A *FUNNY* MAN, MR. KENT.

MAYBE. DO YOU REMEMBER ANY DETAILS ABOUT THESE *FLYING* MEN YOU FOUGHT?

REMEMBER THEM? I'LL REMEMBER THEM TILL I *DIE!*

...I SEE. YES, WELL, KEEP LOOKING. THIS IS YOUR TOP PRIORITY!

DAMN! ALL THESE MEN ...CONTACTS... AND THERE'S NOT A CLUE ABOUT THE BELT!

IT'S TOO VALUABLE TO HIDE. YOU'LL HEAR...

OF COURSE, I'LL HEAR! IT MAGNIFIES NATURAL META-HUMAN TENDENCIES A THOUSAND TIMES!

WHEN IT'S SOLD TO SOMEONE ELSE, I'LL HEAR! WHEN WORD IS LEAKED TO THE MEN I'VE ALREADY PROMISED IT TO, I'LL HEAR! WHEN...

BRRRRIINNGG

YES?

IT'S SORAYA NASSUR, MR. LUTHOR. I WORK FOR YOU, IN SECTION 2, AND, WELL, I MAY HAVE SOME INFORMATION...

I MEAN, OF COURSE I HAVE SOME INFORMATION. I HAVE THE THING ITSELF... SEE, I WAS WORKING LATE LAST NIGHT...

ANYWAY, I FOUND THIS BELT... MY BROTHER AND I DID...

AND WE DON'T WANT IT. REALLY. WE JUST WANT TO GIVE IT BACK. WE KNOW IT'S NOT OURS.

WE JUST DON'T WANT THERE TO BE ANY TROUBLE.

THERE WON'T BE, WILL THERE?

OF COURSE NOT, DEAR GIRL. YOU HAVE MY WORD ON IT.

AND THEN THIS HUGE "GLOWING BALL" SHOT INTO THE SKY?

YES. I'M SURPRISED THAT NEITHER OF THE TWO MEN WHO SUPERMAN CAPTURED YESTERDAY TOLD YOU ANYTHING ABOUT IT.

THEY'RE STILL IN INTENSIVE CARE. BUT--

EARTHQUAKE!

KRRRUMBLE

NO. AN EXPLOSION OF SOME TYPE... ON THE FLOOR BELOW US...

FORTUNATELY, I CAN SEE THROUGH THE FLOOR...

AND WHAT I SEE IS PRETTY BAD...

THAT... ER, SOUNDED LIKE IT CAME FROM THE FLOOR WHERE THE PRISONERS ARE BEING HELD!

CALL THE POLICE! I'M GOING DOWN!

BUT...

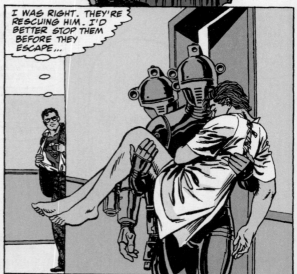

I WAS RIGHT. THEY'RE RESCUING HIM. I'D BETTER STOP THEM BEFORE THEY ESCAPE...

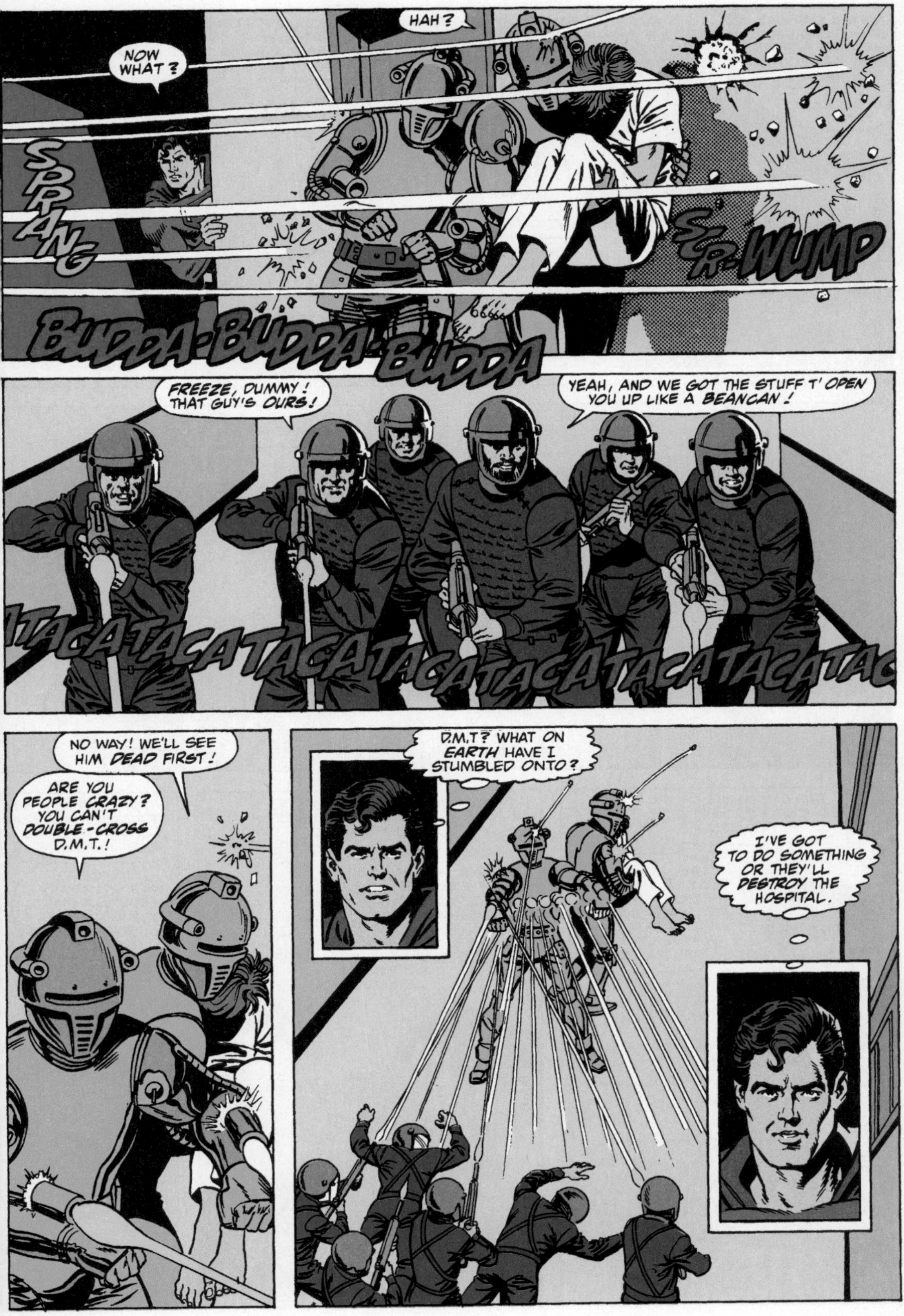

NOW WHAT?
HAH?
SPRANG
SKR-WUMP
BUDDA-BUDDA-BUDDA
FREEZE, DUMMY! THAT GUY'S OURS!
YEAH, AND WE GOT THE STUFF T' OPEN YOU UP LIKE A BEANCAN!
TACATACATACATACATACATACATAC
NO WAY! WE'LL SEE HIM DEAD FIRST!
ARE YOU PEOPLE CRAZY? YOU CAN'T DOUBLE-CROSS D.M.T.!
D.M.T? WHAT ON EARTH HAVE I STUMBLED ONTO?
I'VE GOT TO DO SOMETHING OR THEY'LL DESTROY THE HOSPITAL.

AS YOU CAN SEE, SIR, THE NASSUR GIRL HAS WORKED HERE ABOUT SEVEN MONTHS. HER WORK RECORD IS EXCELLENT, BUT...

...SHE WASN'T DEEMED FLEXIBLE ENOUGH TO WORK ON THE MORE SENSITIVE PROJECTS. I CAN READ, THANK YOU, MS. KREEL.

UH, SIR...?

THERE'S BEEN A CONFLICT AT THE HOSPITAL. SQUAD EPSILON CONTACTED A COUPLE OF D.M.T. BATTLE SUITS. THERE HAVE BEEN CASUALTIES.

MS. NASSUR HAS ARRIVED, SIR...

SHOW HER IN.

AH, MS. NASSUR. SO GOOD TO SEE YOU AGAIN.

I WAS AFRAID YOU WOULDN'T REMEMBER ME, MR. LUTHOR.

NONSENSE. IS THIS THE MERCHANDISE YOU FOUND?

YES, SIR. I CONVINCED MY BROTHER THAT WE SHOULD GIVE IT BACK.

WE'RE SORRY ABOUT THE DAMAGE, BUT WE WERE ATTACKED...

THINK NO MORE OF IT. SO YOUR BROTHER IS THE META-HUMAN?

YES, HE HAS POWERS... HE WAS NERVOUS ABOUT RETURNING THE BELT ...BUT I EXPLAINED WHAT SORT OF MAN YOU WERE...

HOW NICE OF YOU.

GOODWIN, BEGIN TESTS ON THE BELT IMMEDIATELY.

TAKE THE WOMAN TO OUR EUROPEAN COMPLEX. LOSE HER.

AND PICK UP THE BROTHER. WE'LL NEED HIM FOR THE EXPERIMENTS.

NO... NO!

UNFORTUNATELY, MY DEAR, YOU AND YOUR BROTHER ARE LIKE FLIES IN AMBER...

...INNOCENTS WITH NO COMPRE-HENSION OF THAT INTO WHICH THEY HAVE BLUNDERED ...UTTERLY...

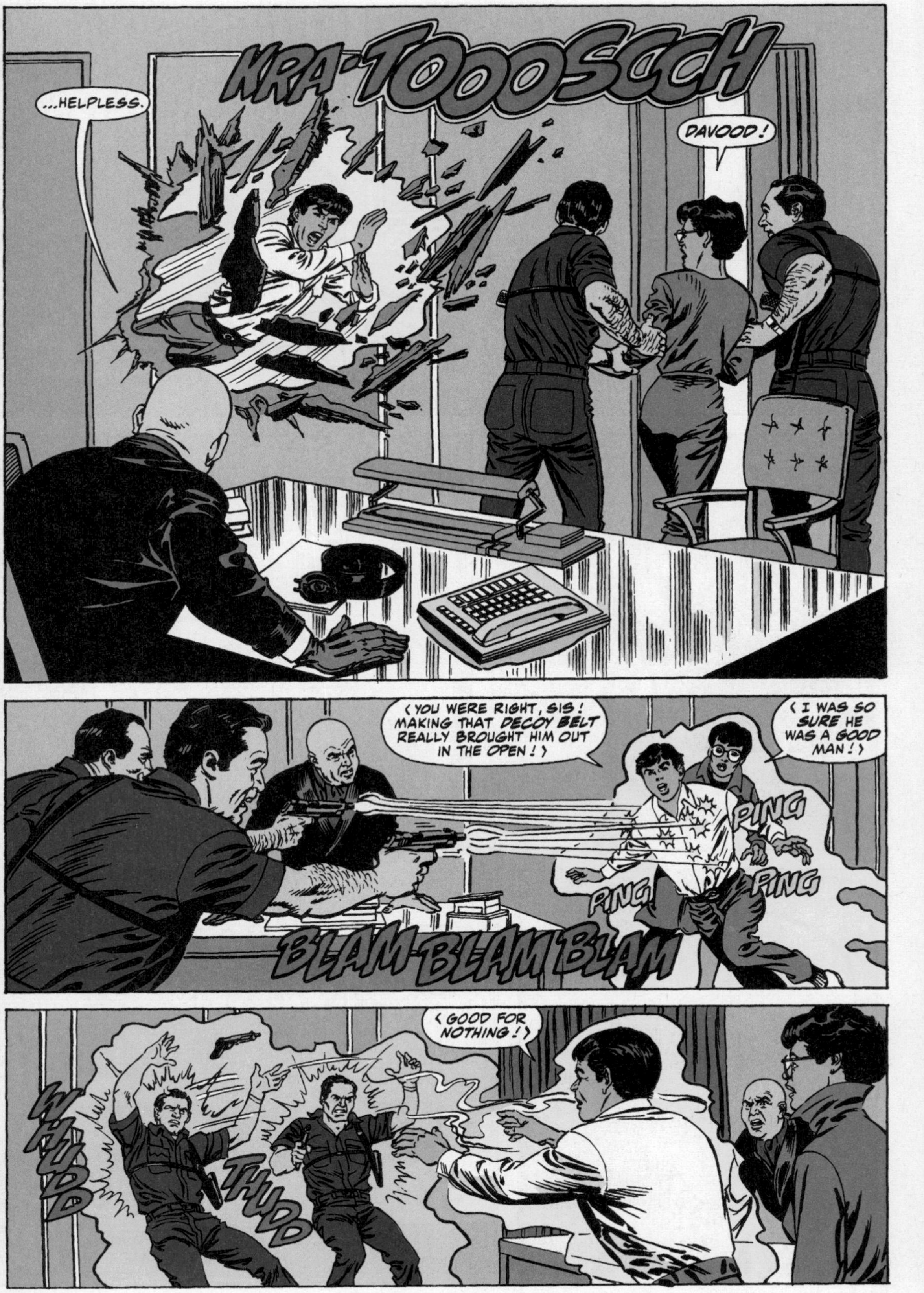
KRA-TOOOSCCH
...HELPLESS.
DAVOOD!
<YOU WERE RIGHT, SIS! MAKING THAT DECOY BELT REALLY BROUGHT HIM OUT IN THE OPEN!>
<I WAS SO SURE HE WAS A GOOD MAN!>
PING
PING
PING
BLAM BLAM BLAM
<GOOD FOR NOTHING!>
WHUD
THUDD

YOU TRIED TO HURT MY SISTER, PIG! DIDN'T YOU THINK THE BELT WOULD LET ME SEE AND HEAR THROUGH WALLS?

NO, BUT I'LL KEEP IT IN MIND FOR THE FUTURE.

ASSUMING YOU *HAVE* A FUTURE.

BE CAREFUL, YOUNG MAN... YOU ARE TRESPA--

STUPID, *GREEDY* OLD MAN.

‹ C'MON, SIS, WE'RE GONE! ›

UNFORTUNATE...

NOW I'LL HAVE TO HAVE THAT OFFENSIVE YOUNG MAN PUT OUT OF COMMISSION.

THIS SAYS HIS FAMILY ARE ARABS, FROM QURAC.

THAT COULD BE *USEFUL.* VERY USEFUL.

IF THIS GOES ON MUCH LONGER, THE BUILDING FOUNDATION WILL COLLAPSE, KILLING HUNDREDS.

A DISTRACTION WOULD BREAK THIS STALEMATE...

BLAM BLAM WHUMP

IF I APPEAR, IT'LL MEAN MORE FIGHTING. BUT IF I CAN KICK UP A CLOUD OF THIS PLASTER DUST...

FROOOSHH

COFF-COFF WHERE'D HE GO?

I'M OUTTA HERE! SO LONG, IDIOTS!

JOHNNY! IS THAT YOU, JOHNNY? I NEVER TOLD 'EM A THING ABOUT THE D.M.T. HONEST. I'VE BEEN QUIET.

GOOD. THAT'S WHAT THEY SENT ME TO FIND OUT...

...AND TO ALSO KEEP YOU QUIET. SORRY, DAVE.

AAHH...HHH

NOW I CAN FOLLOW THEM AT A DISTANCE AND-- WHAT'S HE DOING? OH, NO!

127

‹DAVOOD, WE'VE GOT TO WARN PEOPLE ABOUT MR. LUTHOR... TELL THEM ABOUT THE BELT!›

‹IF WE CALL THE STAR OR THE DAILY PLANET...›

‹ALLAH! THERE'S A MAN FALLING... MILES FROM HERE!›

‹HANG ON, SORAYA!›

‹WHAT DO YOU MEAN, "HANG --?"›

YIIIIIIIIIIIIII!

‹DAVOOD NASSUR! IF YOU EVER DO THAT TO ME AGAIN, I WILL PERSONALLY...›

‹SORRY, SIS! BUT IF I CAN HIT THINGS WITH THIS FORCE FIELD, I SHOULD BE ABLE TO CATCH THINGS, TOO.›

‹LIKE THIS!›

‹BE SURE TO CUSHION HIS FALL.›

‹NAG, NAG, NAG!›

DMT DMT DMT DMT

‹TOO COOL. I CAN SEE WHAT HE'S THINKING!›

< UH ... DAVOOD. COMPANY. >

UHHHHH...

HOLD IT, SON ... I DON'T KNOW WHA--

I AM NOT THE SON OF A MURDERER ...

... AND I'M TIRED OF HOLDING IT, HERE.

< C'MON, SIS. LET'S GO HOME. >

UM, THANKS ...

POIT

HMMM. SO HE CAN TRANSPORT, TOO.

FIRST I HAVE TO GET THIS MAN SOME HELP ... BUT I THINK I KNOW WHERE TO FIND THOSE KIDS.

THAT'S RIGHT, CHIEF. *ARAB TERRORISTS.* THEY BROKE IN HERE, TRASHED MY LAB AND STOLE SEVERAL DEVICES.

IT SEEMS TO BE A WHOLE FAMILY. THE LEADER IS A SAVAGE YOUNG FANATIC WITH *META-HUMAN* POWERS.

I'D *SHOOT* FIRST, IF I WERE YOU.

I CAN GIVE YOU A GOOD DE-SCRIPTION OF HIS COSTUME. HIS NAME...? HE, UH, CALLED HIMSELF *SINBAD!* YES, SINBAD!

"HE EVEN LOOKED LIKE A.... A *PARODY* OF THE LEGENDARY HERO. BUT IN A *HOMEMADE* KIND OF WAY..."

"STILL HE WAS *CRAZED,* I TELL YOU! *INSANE!*"

"HE THREATENED TO BLOW UP BRIDGES AND SCHOOLS AND FACTORIES ALL OVER THE CITY.

DO I THINK HE'LL CARRY THROUGH ON HIS *THREATS?* YES, CAPTAIN SAWYER, I'M REASON-ABLY CERTAIN HE WILL ...

"...NO ... *ABSOLUTELY* CERTAIN."

‹SO MR. LUTHOR IS A BAD MAN?›

‹YEAH, LOOKS LIKE IT. I GUESS I'LL KEEP THE BELT AND, WELL, BECOME A HERO.›

‹MODEST.›

‹DO YOU WANT ME TO SEW YOU A COSTUME, WITH A CAPE AND A NICE MASK?›

‹A COSTUME'S THE LAST THING I NEED, MOM. I'M TOO MUCH OF A TARGET ALREADY.›

‹I ONLY ASKED. EAT YOUR LAMB.›

‹I'M TOO EXCITED TO EAT! YOU SHOULD HAVE SEEN ME!›

‹BOOM! RIGHT THROUGH THE WALL! AND I CAN READ MINDS!›

‹IF YOU CAN READ MINDS, READ MINE AND SEE WHAT WILL HAPPEN IF YOU DON'T EAT LUNCH!›

‹I'M EATING!›

‹AND YOU REALLY TELEPORTED BACK HERE, SORAYA? THAT IS THE MOST TERRIBLE POWER YET!›

‹SURE. AND DAVOOD REALLY DID READ THIS GUY'S MIND.›

‹COULD HE DRAW THE FACE HE SAW?›

‹SURE, I CAN. JUST...›

‹OOPS.›

FRRRSSS

‹GEEZ. I CHARRED THE PAPER...›

‹DO YOU KNOW HIM, UNCLE JAHIR?›

‹YES, I KNOW HIM.›

‹THAT NOISE. THERE IS TROUBLE ON THE STREET.›

OUTSIDE OVER LITTLE QURAC....

THOSE KIDS WERE SPEAKING WHAT SOUNDED LIKE ARABIC....

...AND I HAVE THE NAME ON THE SIDE OF THEIR TRUCK. I'LL JUST ASK AROUND AND...

IRAQI RESTAURANT

WHAT...?

TONNK

HEY! WHAT IS THIS?

GET BACK!

GET OUT OF HERE!

BULLY!

YOU CAN'T SMASH OUR HOMES HERE LIKE YOU DID IN QURAC!

BUTCHER!

I NEVER THOUGHT MY ATTACK ON QURAC A WHILE BACK WOULD BEAR THIS KIND OF FRUIT!

IF I TRY TO STAY, THERE'LL BE A RIOT. SOMEONE WILL BE KILLED...

THIS LOOKS LIKE A JOB...

...FOR CLARK KENT. NOW LET'S FIGURE OUT WHAT'S GOING ON.

EXCUSE ME, MA'AM. I'M CLARK KENT FROM THE *PLANET.* COULD I ASK YOU A COUPLE OF QUESTIONS ABOUT...?

HEY, YOU! CUT THAT *OUT!*

HEY, YOU! BIG MAN! WHAT YOU DOING THERE?

YOU'RE A *FUNNY GUY!* YOU *LIKE* BOTHERING WOMEN ON THE STREET?

NO, NO. I'M A *REPORTER,* AND...

SO... A REPORTER. YOU CAME DOWN HERE TO WRITE *LIES* ABOUT US WHILE *SUPERMAN* SMASHES OUR NEIGHBORHOOD? PIG!

NO...! I CAN'T GET AWAY, AND IF I START TO BRAWL WITH SO MANY I'LL HAVE TO USE MY *SUPER-STRENGTH...*

WHAT CAN I *DO?*

BRIITT BRIITT CLK

GOODWIN ... MY CAR.

AT LAST. A BREAK IN THIS SORRY MESS.

THERE'S NO POINT IN MY *PRETEND-ING* RELUCTANCE THEY *KNOW* MY NEEDS... JUST AS I KNOW THEIRS.

HELLO, SIR. WHERE --?

I'LL DIRECT YOU AS WE GO.

LEFT AT THIS CORNER.

STILL, THEY ARE BEING VERY *DIRECT.* I WONDER WHAT THAT DIRECT-NESS *HIDES?*

YES? WHO? HOW DID YOU GET THIS--? I SEE. YES, I SEE.

I'LL BE THERE IN TWENTY MINUTES.

INTERESTING. THIS WAREHOUSE IS *SUPPOSED* TO BE A CIA DROP.

BUT *I* ACTUALLY OWN IT THROUGH A SERIES OF INTERLOCKING COMPANIES...

AND YET *THEY* HAVE MANAGED TO *COVERTLY* USE IT. I'M IMPRESSED.

MY NAME IS LUTHOR. YOU ASKED TO SEE ME? SOMETHING ABOUT A *TRUCE*?

INDEED YES, MR. LUTHOR. BEFORE OUR FEUD BECOMES ANY MORE *PUBLIC*, NEITHER OF US DESIRES THAT.

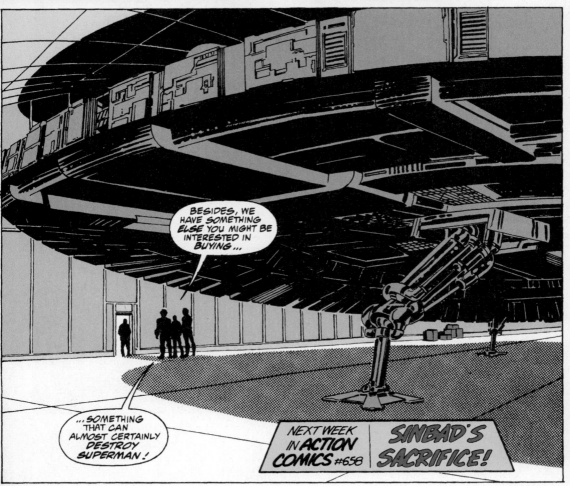

BESIDES, WE HAVE SOMETHING ELSE YOU MIGHT BE INTERESTED IN BUYING...

...SOMETHING THAT CAN ALMOST CERTAINLY DESTROY SUPERMAN!

NEXT WEEK IN *ACTION COMICS* #658 | *SINBAD'S SACRIFICE!*

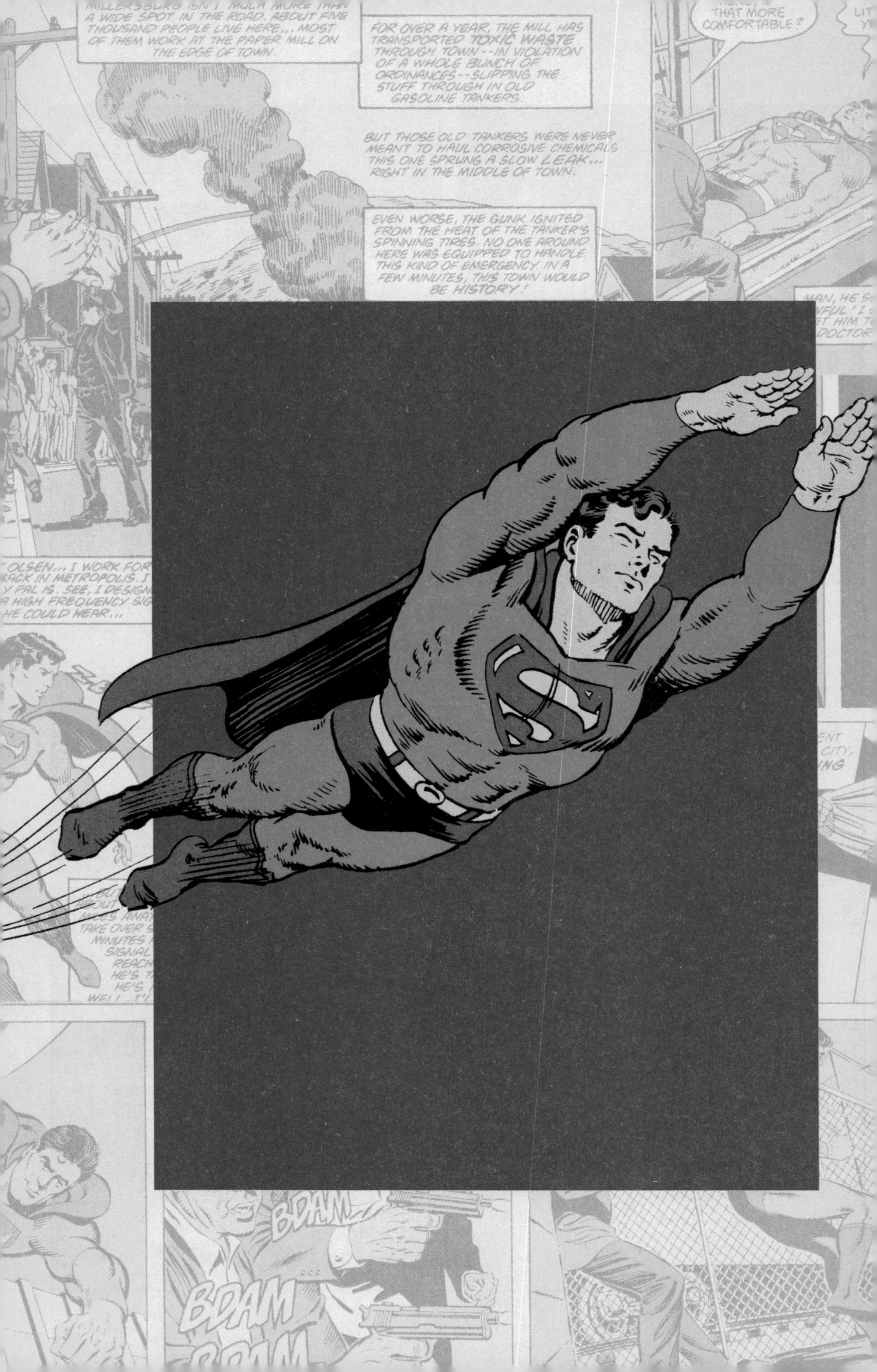

A WIDE SPOT IN THE ROAD. ABOUT FIVE THOUSAND PEOPLE LIVE HERE... MOST OF THEM WORK AT THE PAPER MILL ON THE EDGE OF TOWN.
FOR OVER A YEAR, THE MILL HAS TRANSPORTED TOXIC WASTE THROUGH TOWN--IN VIOLATION OF A WHOLE BUNCH OF ORDINANCES--SLIPPING THE STUFF THROUGH IN OLD GASOLINE TANKERS.
THAT MORE COMFORTABLE?
BUT THOSE OLD TANKERS WERE NEVER MEANT TO HAUL CORROSIVE CHEMICALS. THIS ONE SPRUNG A SLOW LEAK... RIGHT IN THE MIDDLE OF TOWN.
EVEN WORSE, THE GUNK IGNITED FROM THE HEAT OF THE TANKER'S SPINNING TIRES. NO ONE AROUND HERE WAS EQUIPPED TO HANDLE THIS KIND OF EMERGENCY. IN A FEW MINUTES, THIS TOWN WOULD BE HISTORY!
BDAM
BDAM

Cover art by Kerry Gammill and Bob McLeod.

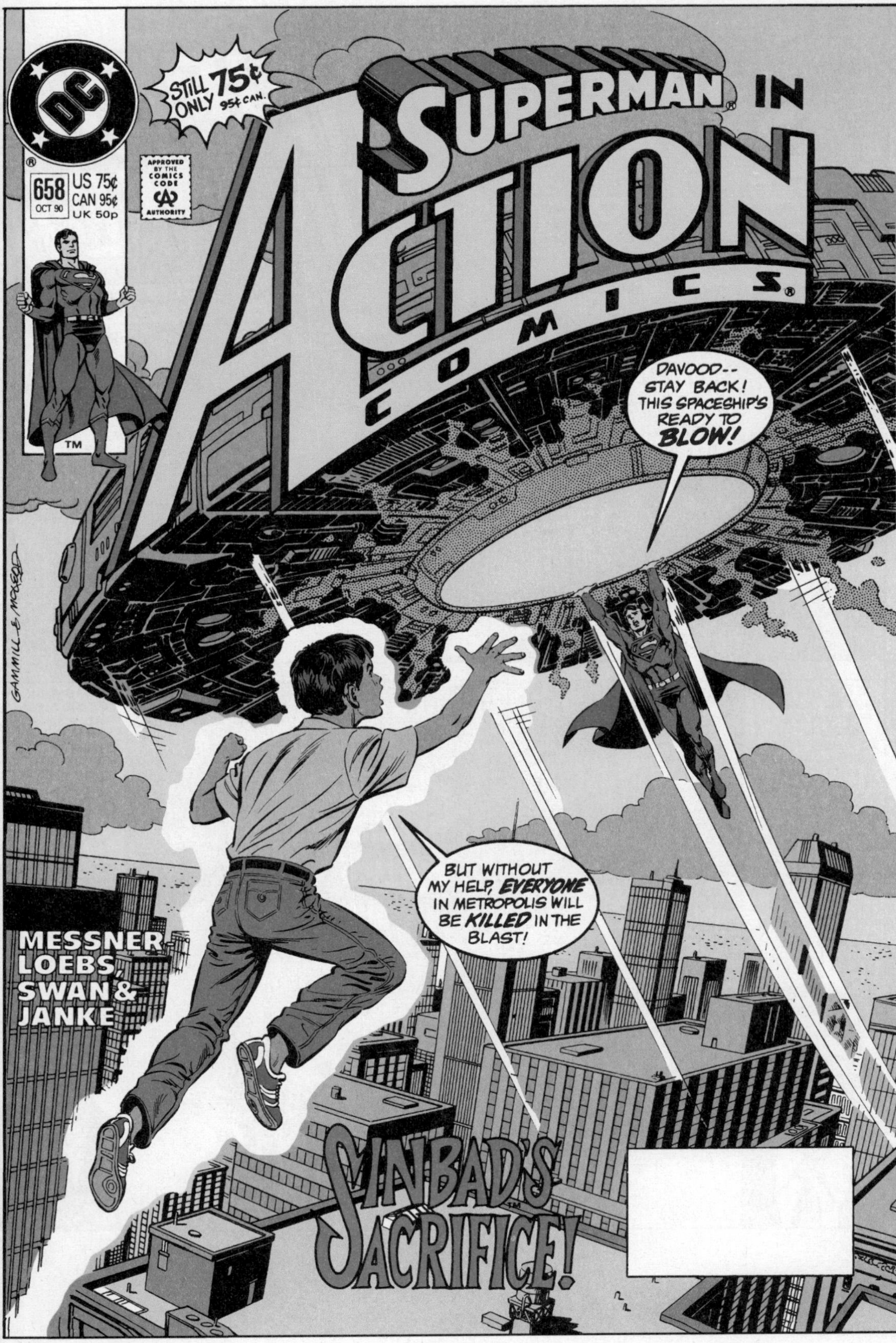

STILL ONLY 75¢ 95¢ CAN.
658 OCT 90
US 75¢ CAN 95¢ UK 50p
APPROVED BY THE COMICS CODE AUTHORITY
SUPERMAN IN ACTION COMICS
DAVOOD-- STAY BACK! THIS SPACESHIP'S READY TO BLOW!
BUT WITHOUT MY HELP, EVERYONE IN METROPOLIS WILL BE KILLED IN THE BLAST!
MESSNER-LOEBS, SWAN & JANKE
SINBAD'S SACRIFICE!
GAMMILL & McLEOD

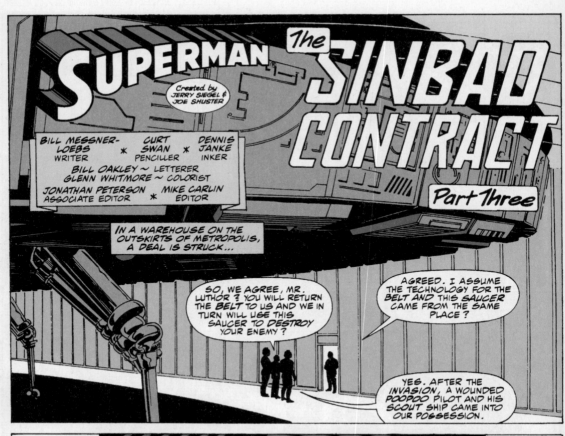

SUPERMAN The SINBAD CONTRACT

Created by
JERRY SIEGEL &
JOE SHUSTER

Part Three

BILL MESSNER-LOEBS — WRITER * CURT SWAN — PENCILLER * DENNIS JANKE — INKER
BILL OAKLEY ~ LETTERER
GLENN WHITMORE ~ COLORIST
JONATHAN PETERSON — ASSOCIATE EDITOR * MIKE CARLIN — EDITOR

IN A WAREHOUSE ON THE OUTSKIRTS OF METROPOLIS, A DEAL IS STRUCK...

SO, WE AGREE, MR. LUTHOR? YOU WILL RETURN THE BELT TO US AND WE IN TURN WILL USE THIS SAUCER TO DESTROY YOUR ENEMY?

AGREED. I ASSUME THE TECHNOLOGY FOR THE BELT AND THIS SAUCER CAME FROM THE SAME PLACE?

YES. AFTER THE INVASION, A WOUNDED POOPOO PILOT AND HIS SCOUT SHIP CAME INTO OUR POSSESSION.

WE... CONVINCED HIM TO WORK FOR US ON VARIOUS DEVICES FOR SEVERAL MONTHS.

EVENTUALLY, HE DIED. THE BELT WAS HIS MOST ADVANCED PROJECT. WE CANNOT DUPLICATE IT.

SO WHEN YOUR AGENT...

MISLAID...

MISLAID THE BELT, YOU CAN UNDERSTAND OUR DISTRESS.

NATURALLY.

BUT NOW I UNDERSTAND YOU NO LONGER POSSESS THE BELT?

THAT IS BEING REMEDIED. THE YOUNG MAN WHO TOOK THE BELT FROM ME WILL SOON REGRET HIS RASHNESS.

EVEN NOW, I AM TAKING STEPS TO ASSURE THAT NO ONE WILL SHELTER OR BELIEVE HIM. NO ONE!

WHILE IN LITTLE QURAC, TEMPERS ARE ALREADY RUNNING HIGH...

NOW, WAIT A SECOND. I'M JUST TRYING TO GET SOME INFORMATION...

I CAN'T CHANGE TO SUPERMAN... AND I DON'T WANT TO FIGHT THESE MEN...

GET OUT OF HERE! WE KNOW THE SORT OF LIES YOU WANT TO TELL ABOUT US!

‹ STOP IT, RAFFIR! ›

‹ ARE YOU INSANE? WHAT ARE YOU DOING ATTACKING THIS MAN? DO YOU WANT TO ROT IN JAIL? ›

‹ I WANT JUSTICE! IF WE BREAK A FEW OF THESE LIARS' HEADS, THEY'LL LEARN... ›

‹ LEARN WHAT? THAT YOU'RE AN IDIOT? ›

‹ I THOUGHT YOU'D KNOW BETTER THAN TO BUCKLE UNDER TO THESE PEOPLE, TIMUR! ›

‹ I DON'T HAVE TO PROVE MY COURAGE... LEAST OF ALL TO YOU! ›

UM... THANKS.

RAFFIR'S ALWAYS BEEN A HOTHEAD.

I RECOGNIZE YOU FROM THE PAPER. YOU WRITE A COLUMN, YES?

YES. MY NAME'S KENT. ACTUALLY, I'M LOOKING FOR A COUPLE OF KIDS...

I THINK THEY WORK IN THAT GROCERY STORE AND THEY MAY BE IN TROUBLE.

I SEE. THEN MAYBE GOD SENT YOU AFTER ALL. COME ON.

NO PARKING 6 A.M. TO 7 P.M.

IT'S AMAZING THAT JUST AN APPEARANCE BY *SUPERMAN* COULD CAUSE SUCH A RUCKUS.

NOT THAT AMAZING. WE SAW HOW HE *ATTACKED QURACIS* AS THOUGH THEY WERE NOTHING...

INVADED A COUNTRY AND *DESTROYED* THEIR *SOVEREIGNTY!* HE IS THE *ENEMY* OF ARABS EVERY-WHERE.

HE'D HAVE TO BE A FOOL NOT TO REALIZE HOW WE FEEL ABOUT HIM.

YES. I GUESS HE'D HAVE TO BE.

MOTI, I HAVE SOMEONE WE SHOULD TALK TO. TELL *DAVOOD* AND *SORAYA* TO COME HERE.

I CAN'T. THEY'RE GONE.

WHEN HE HEARD THERE WERE GOVERNMENT MEN LOOKING FOR HIM THROUGH THE NEIGHBORHOOD, HE KNEW HE HAD TO GO.

SORAYA WENT WITH HIM. SHE SAYS THAT THEY MUST *PROVE* HE IS *NOT* THIS "SINBAD" TERRORIST.

I AM SO AFRAID FOR THEM. NO ONE WILL BELIEVE US THAT HE IS *INNOCENT.*

MR. LUTHOR IS AGAINST US. *SUPERMAN* IS AGAINST US! WHO CAN WE TRUST?

I...

LISTEN! IT IS ANOTHER *REPORT!*

...A SPECIAL REPORT...

...HAS BEEN ANOTHER SIGHTING OF THE MYSTERIOUS TERRORIST CALLING HIMSELF "SINBAD"--

--THIS TIME IN CONJUNCTION WITH THE BOMBING OF THE METROPOLIS WATER TREATMENT FACILITY.

NEWS

FORTUNATELY, THERE WAS LITTLE DAMAGE AND NO CASUALTIES.

POLICE CONSIDER SINBAD A META-HUMAN AND EXTREMELY DANGEROUS.

THIS JUST IN. SINBAD HAS BEEN IDENTIFIED AS "DAVOOD NASSUR," A QURACI WITH KNOWN RADICAL TIES.

POLICE ARE ADVISING EXTREME CAUTION...

WE HAVE TO FIGURE OUT WHAT'S GOING ON. ARE YOU SURE THOSE WERE GOVERNMENT MEN?

ALLAH, NO! THEY'LL KILL HIM!

WHO ELSE WOULD THEY BE?

I'M NOT SURE... BUT WITH LEXCORP INVOLVED...

HOLD IT RIGHT THERE!

THIS IS THE RESIDENCE OF DAVOOD NASSUR? WE HAVE SOME QUESTIONS TO ASK YOU.

I'D ADVISE YOU TO COOPERATE.

BUT WHAT IS THIS ABOUT? WE DON'T KNOW ANYTHING.

THAT'S NOT MY BUSINESS, SIR. YOU'VE ALL GOT TO COME IN FOR QUESTIONING. PLEASE COME RIGHT AWAY.

COULD I SEE SOME I.D., OFFICER? YOU ARE WITH THE POLICE?

WE'RE HELPING THE POLICE. THIS ISN'T YOUR BUSINESS, FRIEND. BUY YOUR GUMBALLS AND MOVE ALONG.

THESE PEOPLE ARE CITIZENS. YOU CAN'T JUST--

THIS AREA'S SORT OF UNDER MARTIAL LAW UNTIL DAVOOD NASSUR IS FOUND.

KEEP Y'R NOSE OUT OF THIS AND YOU WON'T GET HURT!

PLEASE, DON'T GET YOURSELF IN TROUBLE. WE MUST OBEY THE AUTHOR-ITIES. IT WILL BE ALL RIGHT.

I'M NOT CONVINCED THESE ARE "THE AUTHORITIES." SO ONCE I LET THEM TAKE YOU AWAY...

... I'LL HAVE TO ACT QUICKLY... BEFORE THEY CAN GET THEIR GUNS OUT. RIGHT--

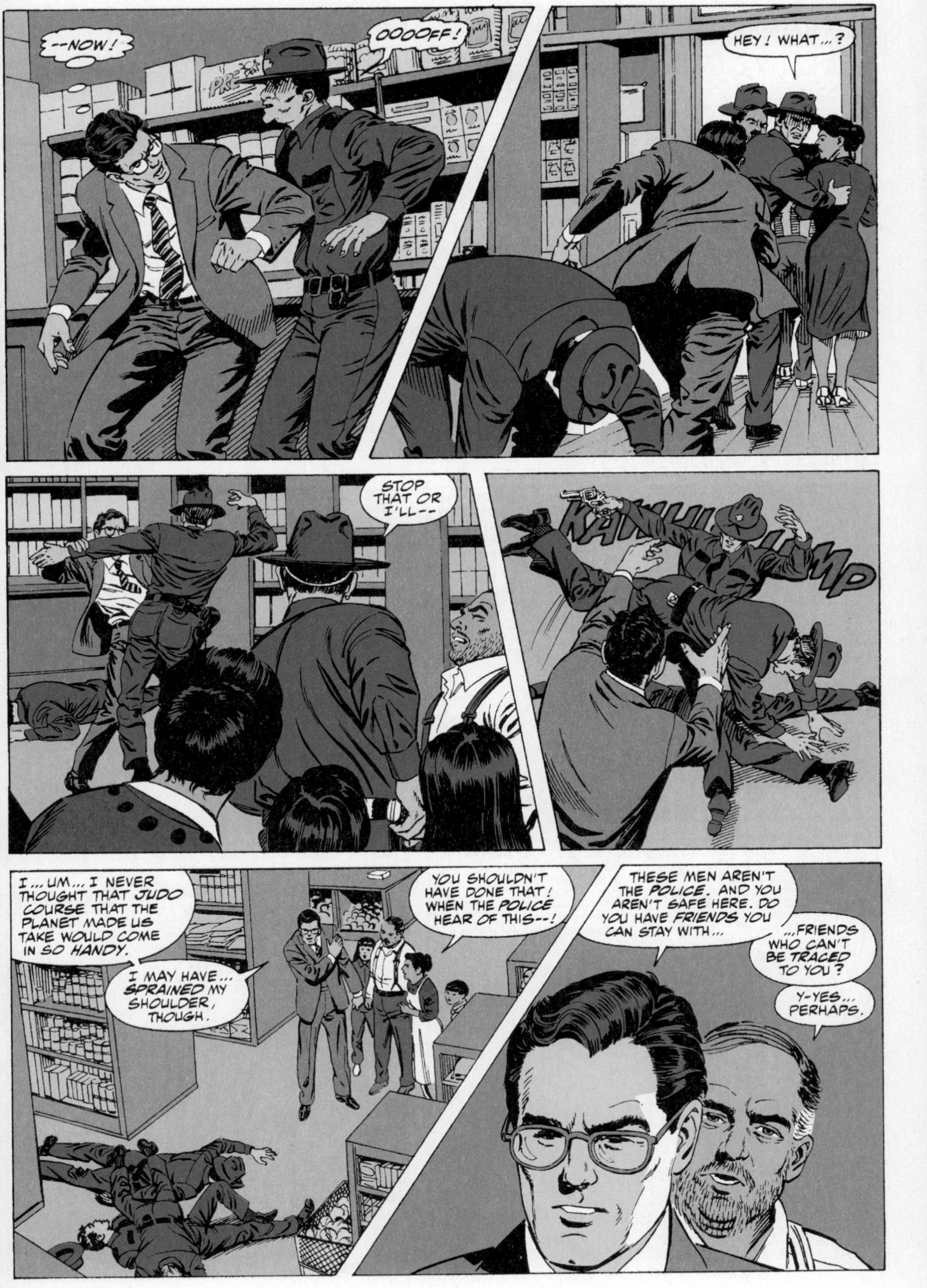
--NOW!
OOOOFF!
HEY! WHAT...?
STOP THAT OR I'LL--
I... UM... I NEVER THOUGHT THAT JUDO COURSE THAT THE PLANET MADE US TAKE WOULD COME IN SO HANDY.
I MAY HAVE... SPRAINED MY SHOULDER, THOUGH.
YOU SHOULDN'T HAVE DONE THAT! WHEN THE POLICE HEAR OF THIS--!
THESE MEN AREN'T THE POLICE. AND YOU AREN'T SAFE HERE. DO YOU HAVE FRIENDS YOU CAN STAY WITH...
...FRIENDS WHO CAN'T BE TRACED TO YOU?
Y-YES... PERHAPS.

"I HAVE A FEELING THINGS ARE ABOUT TO BLOW WIDE OPEN!"

RUN THE *TIMER* WIRE AROUND THE OUTSIDE.

HOW MUCH TIME DO WE WANT IT SET FOR *THIS* TIME?

A QUARTER OF AN HOUR. WE GOTTA RUN AROUND FRONT, GET SEEN, THEN "FLY OFF."

THIS *EVIL* SINBAD GUY'LL GET THE BLAME...

'SPECIALLY 'CAUSE HE'S GONNA ACTUALLY *BLOW UP* SOMEBODY THIS TIME.

NOW, IS THAT *NICE*?

I MEAN, HERE WE ARE, TWO *HOUNDED*, PATHETIC *FUGITIVES* AND YOU'RE MAKING UP *STORIES* ABOUT US! NAUGHTY!

SHE'S NUTS! WASTE HER!

PING PING PING PING

⟨HA! THEY LOOK *SCARED*!⟩

⟨SO DO I! YOU WAITED TOO LONG TO SHIELD ME! I COULD'VE BEEN *KILLED*!⟩

⟨*SISTERS*!⟩

⟨HEY! THESE *THREADS* ARE PRETTY COOL!⟩

⟨RIGHT. IF YOU LIVE IN A *CIRCUS*!⟩

NOW LISTEN *CAREFULLY*, BOZO! WE HAVE A MESSAGE FOR *MR. LUTHOR*...!

There's been another bomb-ing!

That's the THIRD one today!

Someone should DO something!

I hear they're gonna call out the National Guard and SWEEP the Quraci Quarter for this SINBAD. About TIME!

That's RIGHT! I hear that Lex Luthor has volunteered his SECURITY team to PATROL public buildings.

Yes. Yes, I see. That's INTEREST-ING. Thanks, Chief. I owe you one...

Lexcorp claims it doesn't have men in the Quraci Quarter...

That's probably a LIE. But where can Davood and his sister be? It's almost as if--

I think we should just send SUPERMAN in there.

He'll clean 'em out, just like he cleaned out those TOWEL-HEADS in QURAC!

RIGHT, KENT?

If you give Superman that kind of POWER, Timmons, you'll have created a far worse TERRORIST than any he could SMASH.

HUH! Get off it, Kent! We ALL know that neigh-borhood BREEDS terrorists and CRIME.

What we need is someone like Gotham has-- a BATMAN-- to wipe it out!

The BATMAN'S not a RACIST or a FOOL, Timmons, and that puts him miles ahead of you.

MR. KENT? You've got a MESSAGE!

He said his name was "HENRY" and that he'd be feeding the pigeons in the usual place. Does that mean something?

I hope so, Alice. I really do.

I STILL DO NOT SEE *HOW* THESE FAKED *TERRORIST* ATTACKS CAN HELP US RECOVER THE BELT.

BECAUSE PEOPLE ARE BEST CONTROLLED THROUGH *FEAR*. IF I CAN PROVOKE A *RIOT*, WE CAN GO INTO *LITTLE QURAC* WITH GUNS BLAZING.

NO ONE WILL OBJECT!

AND THE LITTLE *SURPRISE* YOU MENTIONED WITHIN THIS MACHINE... IS IT *NUCLEAR*?

THE *NEXT STEP*. IT'S THE *FAIL-SAFE* BUILT IN BY THE ALIENS. VERY POTENT.

ONCE THE BOY AND THE BELT ARE... *TAKEN*, THERE'LL BE NOTHING LEFT TO *INVESTIGATE*.

ALL PEOPLE WILL REMEMBER WAS THERE WAS A *TERRORIST* AND LEXCORP STOPPED HIM.

YOU SEE, ONCE YOU KNOW WHAT PEOPLE *FEAR*, YOU CAN EASILY *CONTROL*...

MR. LUTHOR! HELP!

EH? WHAT ARE YOU DOING HERE? AND *WHERE* ARE YOUR CLOTHES?

SINBAD... THE *REAL SINBAD*... TOOK 'EM! HE GAVE US A MESSAGE!

HE SAID TO TELL YOU HE'S GONNA STOP ALL THE *FAKE SINBADS*... THEN HE'S GONNA TAKE BACK *LITTLE QURAC*...!

AND THEN HE'S COMIN' FOR YOU!

INDEED. THEN I WILL KNOW JUST *WHERE* HE IS.

IF SUPERMAN CAN BE CONVINCED TO BE THIS *PREDICTABLE*...

"...DESTROYING THEM BOTH WILL BE AS SIMPLE AS A WALK IN THE PARK."

AND THERE HE IS. HE DOESN'T LOOK MUCH LIKE A *SPOOK.* I GUESS THAT'S THE POINT.

HELLO, "HENRY." STILL HARD AT WORK, I SEE.

OF COURSE. I LIVE TO SERVE.

ACTUALLY, THERE'S A SORT OF TWIST TO THE WRIST YOU HAVE TO GIVE, TO MAKE THE CRUMBS *ATTRACTIVE...* SORT OF LIKE *MAYFLIES.*

C'MON, TAKE IT, Y'LITTLE *ROOF RATS!*

SO, DID YOU FIND OUT ANYTHING?

NOT MUCH. YOUR BOY IS *CLEAN.* NO TERRORIST CONNECTIONS.

HIS UNCLE WAS A UNION ORGANIZER AGAINST THE *SHAH,* BUT THAT WAS A *LONG* TIME AGO.

INTERESTING. AND YET WE KEEP HEARING HOW THIS KID HAS A *HISTORY OF* TERRORISM. ANY OTHER TIDBITS?

ONLY THAT THERE'S A BUNCH OF *ARMS MERCHANTS* CALLED *R.M.T.* BAD GUYS. THEY'RE HERE IN METROPOLIS. NO CLUE AS TO *WHY.*

C'MON, "HENRY." GIVE. THE *L.I.C.U.D.* KNOWS MORE THAN THAT.

CLARKIE... YOU KEEP INSISTING I'M SOMETHING OTHER THAN A POOR, UNDERPAID *BUREAUCRAT* AT THE *ISRAELI EMBASSY.*

SPIES YOU'VE GOT ON THE *BRAIN!*

AFTER ALL, IT *MIGHT* BE TO *OUR* ADVANTAGE TO LET YOU THINK THIS KID IS SOME KIND OF *SUPER-TERRORIST.*

BUT INSTEAD I FEED YOU THE *STRAIGHT* STUFF. BESIDES...

THIS MAY BE BESIDE THE POINT. THIS SINBAD HAS BEEN SPOTTED IN LITTLE QURAC.

HRM ... WHAT'S THIS?

THERE'S SOME KIND OF *FIREFIGHT* GOING ON. THE POLICE ARE INVOLVED, BUT THE WHOLE SITUATION IS *DIS-INTEGRATING.*

IT SOUNDS LIKE HE'S DONE FOR. WANT TO GIVE A LISTEN?

CLARK? *CLARK?*

NOW, WHERE'D HE GO?

148

"HE ALWAYS ACTS LIKE HE'S ON HIS WAY TO A FIRE!"

EXCUSE ME...SIR?

ARE YOU HERE TO *ARREST* "SINBAD"? DO YOU KNOW *WHERE* HE IS? IS HIS REAL NAME *DAVOOD NASSUR*?

RATS!

AH, CATHERINE GRANT. ANOTHER *NO COMMENT*?

LUTHOR...? WHAT ARE YOU DOING HERE?

JUST BEING A CONCERNED CITIZEN. MY OFFICES WERE ATTACKED, TOO.

FRANKLY, I THINK IT'S VERY *LIKELY* THAT THIS *TERRORIST* WILL APPEAR.

AND IN THAT CASE, WE'LL NEED ALL THE *PROTECTION* WE CAN GET.

NOW, WAIT A SECOND. WE GOT A PHONE CALL FROM SOME-ONE CLAIMING TO BE THIS *SINBAD* CHARACTER.

HE SAID HE WAS GOING TO *DESTROY* A SECTION OF THE CITY TO SHOW HIS *POWER!* BUT WE DON'T EVEN KNOW--

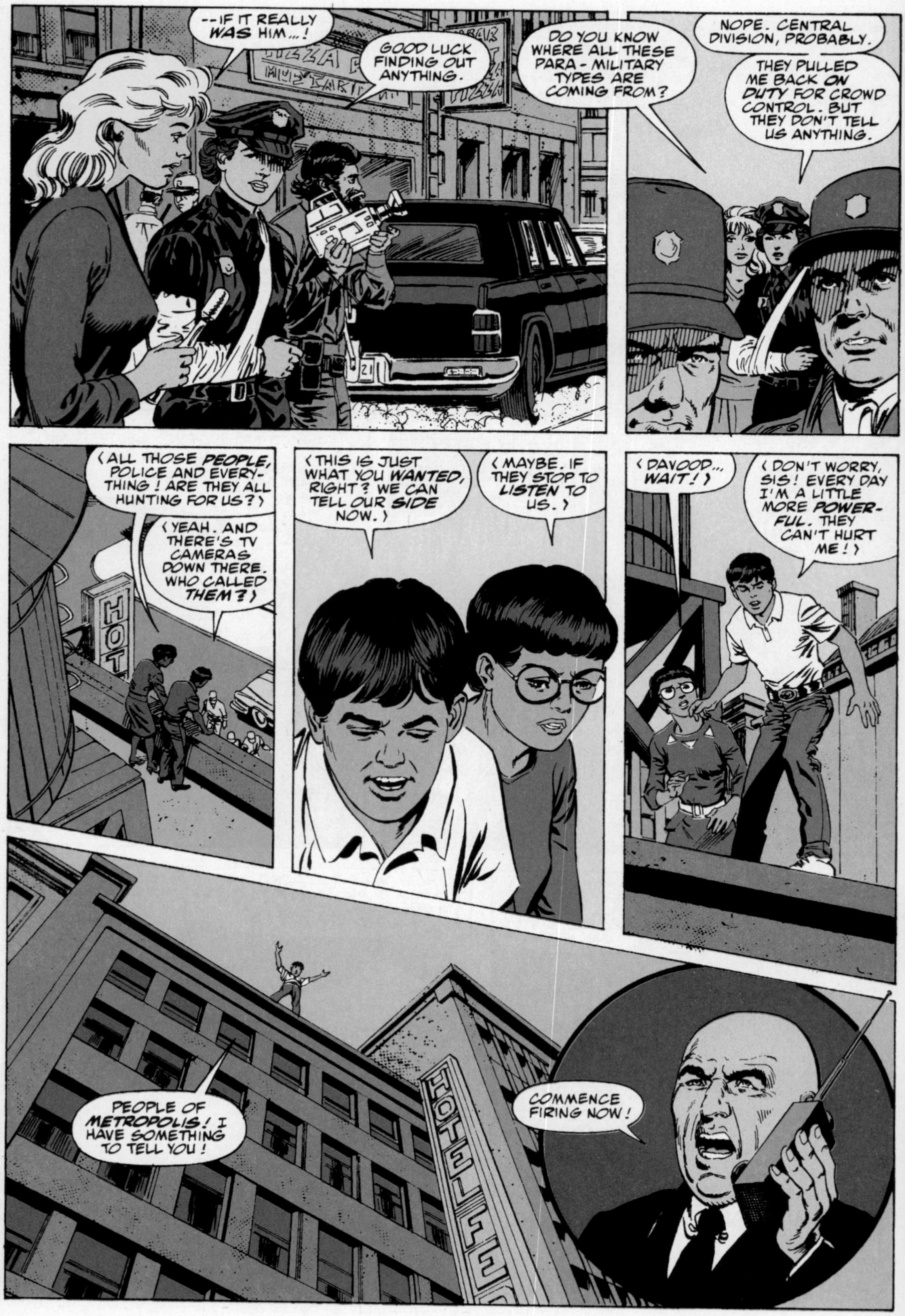
--IF IT REALLY WAS HIM...!
GOOD LUCK FINDING OUT ANYTHING.
DO YOU KNOW WHERE ALL THESE PARA-MILITARY TYPES ARE COMING FROM?
NOPE. CENTRAL DIVISION, PROBABLY.
THEY PULLED ME BACK ON DUTY FOR CROWD CONTROL. BUT THEY DON'T TELL US ANYTHING.
‹ALL THOSE PEOPLE, POLICE AND EVERYTHING! ARE THEY ALL HUNTING FOR US?›
‹YEAH. AND THERE'S TV CAMERAS DOWN THERE. WHO CALLED THEM?›
‹THIS IS JUST WHAT YOU WANTED, RIGHT? WE CAN TELL OUR SIDE NOW.›
‹MAYBE. IF THEY STOP TO LISTEN TO US.›
‹DAVOOD... WAIT!›
‹DON'T WORRY, SIS! EVERY DAY I'M A LITTLE MORE POWERFUL. THEY CAN'T HURT ME!›
PEOPLE OF METROPOLIS! I HAVE SOMETHING TO TELL YOU!
COMMENCE FIRING NOW!

HEY! WHAT ARE YOU GUYS DOING? THERE WASN'T A COMMAND TO--

BRRRAAATTT
BRRRAAATTT
BRRRAAATTT
POOOMM
POOMM

HEY! WHAT'S WRONG WITH YOU PEOPLE?

〈DAVOOD! TEARGAS!〉

〉 COFF-COFF 〈 〈 PUSH IT AWAY, DAVOOD! 〉 〉GASP〈 〈 MAKE IT STOP! 〉

〉COFF〈 〈 I CAN'T! I DON'T KNOW HOW! 〉 〉 GASP 〈 〈 I-I CAN'T SEE... 〉

〈 I CAN'T... BREATHE... HAVE TO GET AWAY... HAVE TO ...NO...! 〉

I WOULDN'T GO DOWN THIS WAY. THERE DON'T SEEM TO BE ANY STAIRS.

〈SUPERMAN!〉

FFWWWOOOOOOOSSHHHHH

FIRST I GET RID OF THE GAS -- THEN THE *SOURCE* OF THE GAS...

AND *NOW* FOR MY NEXT TRICK...

THE THREATS AND THE TEAR-GAS AND THE BULLETS DIDN'T *WORK*, SO THEY SENT *YOU!* CHEW ON THIS!

WHUMP!

DAVOOD!

〈 DON'T BE AN *IDIOT*, DAVOOD! HE'S *NOT* ATTACK-ING US! HE JUST *SAVED MY LIFE!* 〉

〈 WELL, BUT... HE *LOOKED* LIKE HE WAS GONNA START SOMETHING! 〉

BROTHER, THERE'S *NO WAY* I WANT TO FIGHT HIM! HE JUST ABOUT TOOK MY HEAD OFF!

ALL I WANT TO FIGURE OUT IS--

LOOK! UP THERE!

MY GOD! IT'S THAT...

...THE "UFO!"

NOW WE'LL SEE HOW POWERFUL A WEAPON THIS SAUCER REALLY IS, GOODWIN.

YES, IT'S SUPPOSED TO BE POWERFUL ENOUGH TO SLICE SUPERMAN IN HALF, LIKE AN APPLE!

LET'S SEE, SHALL WE?

IS IT GOING TO SHOOT AT US?

NO WAY TO TELL...

AT LEAST *YOU* DON'T HAVE TO BE AFRAID. YOU'RE *INVULNERABLE.*

SHELLS AND BULLETS AND LASER BEAMS ALWAYS *BOUNCE* OFF YOU.

THEY HAVE UP TILL NOW. BUT THERE'S *NO* GUARANTEE...

"I THINK I'LL SEE JUST WHO'S INSIDE THAT..."

"THERE'S NO ONE INSIDE! IT'S A *ROBOT SHIP!*"

"BUT... WHY?"

"WAIT! IT'S BEEN SET TO EXPLODE!"

"IT'S A *BOMB!*"

00:04

I'VE GOT TO GET THIS AWAY FROM THE CITY!

WHAT THE *DEVIL?*

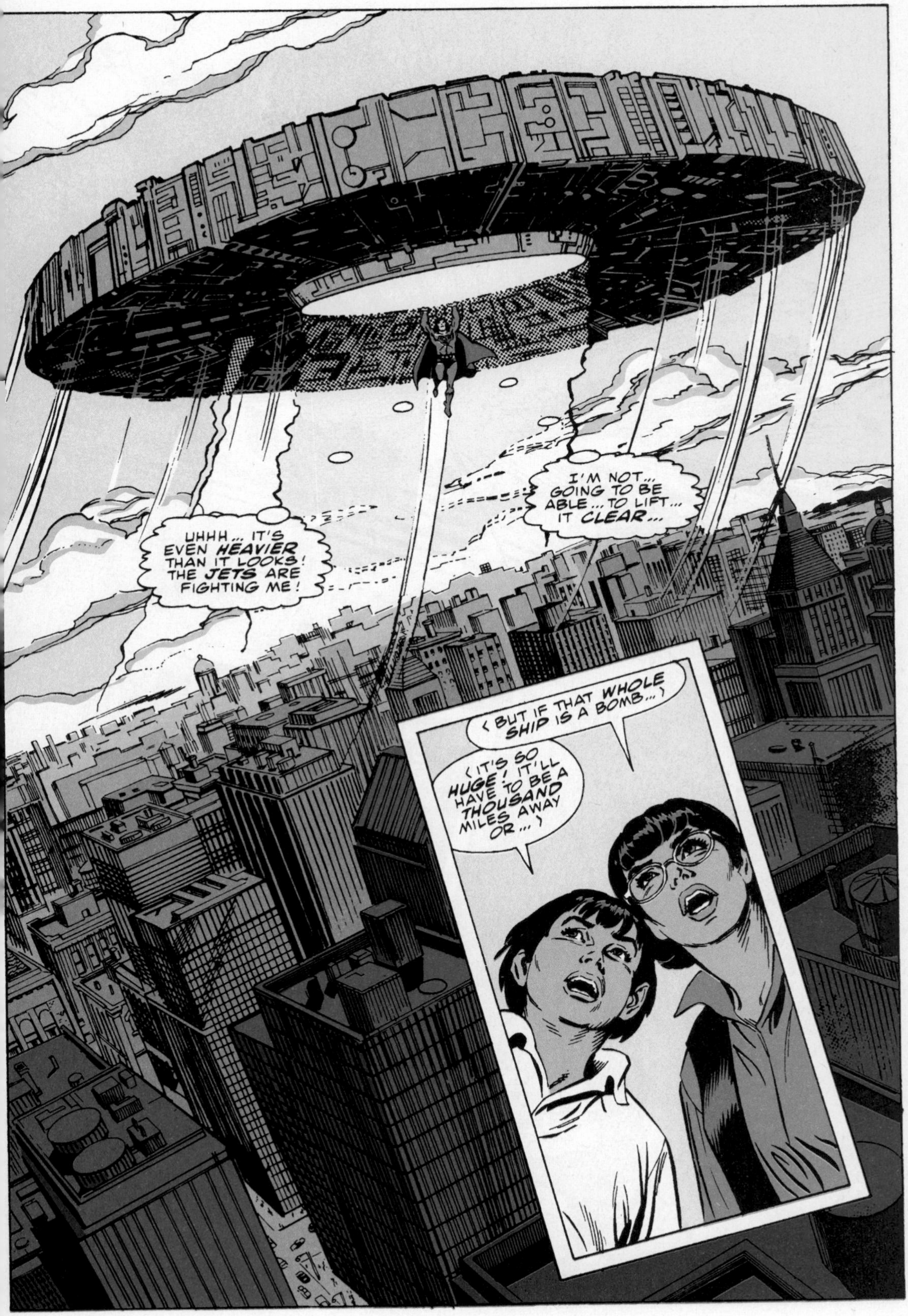
UHHH... IT'S EVEN HEAVIER THAN IT LOOKS! THE JETS ARE FIGHTING ME!
I'M NOT... GOING TO BE ABLE... TO LIFT... IT CLEAR...
‹ BUT IF THAT WHOLE SHIP IS A BOMB... ›
‹ IT'S SO HUGE! IT'LL HAVE TO BE A THOUSAND MILES AWAY OR... ›

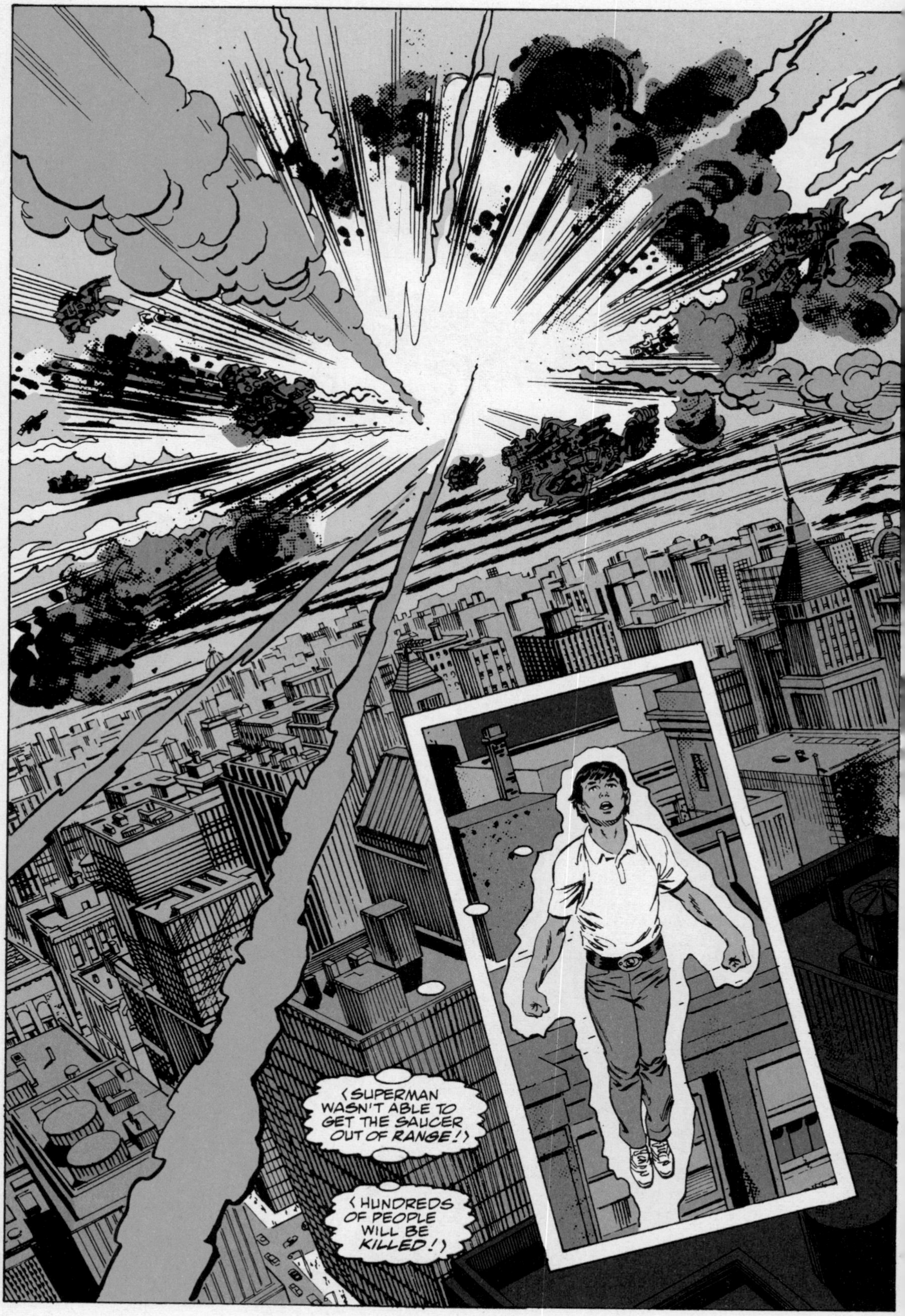
‹SUPERMAN WASN'T ABLE TO GET THE SAUCER OUT OF RANGE!›
‹HUNDREDS OF PEOPLE WILL BE KILLED!›

(I CAN'T LET THE *FORCE* OF THE EXPLOSION *TOUCH* THE EARTH!)

(MY SHIELD HAS TO BE LARGER...)

(LARGER...)

(I....I.... DID IT!)

DID IT....

'COURSE YOU DID.

DRIVE. GET ME TO MY TELEVISION STATION. QUICKLY.

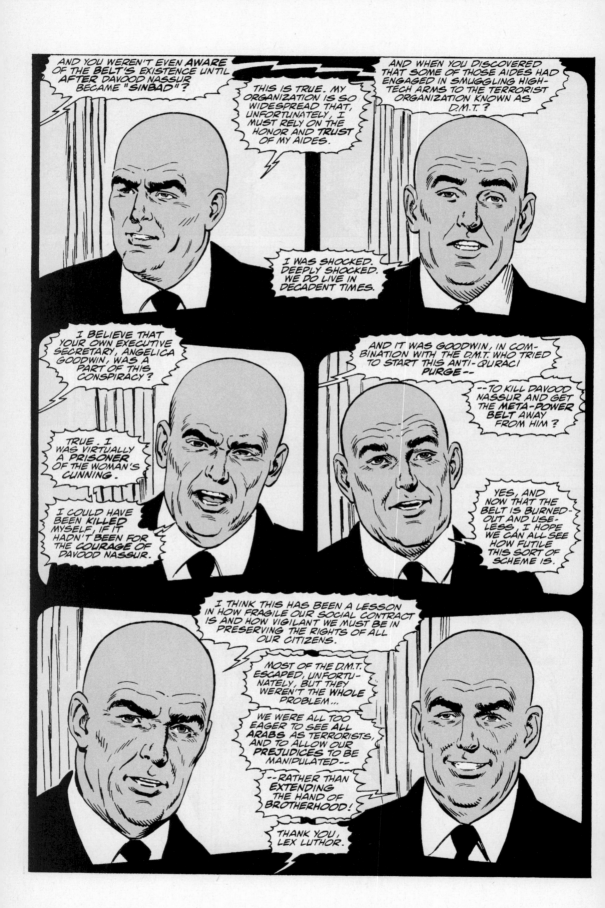

AND YOU WEREN'T EVEN *AWARE* OF THE *BELT'S* EXISTENCE UNTIL AFTER DAVOOD NASSUR BECAME "*SINBAD*"?

THIS IS TRUE. MY ORGANIZATION IS SO WIDESPREAD THAT, UNFORTUNATELY, I MUST RELY ON THE HONOR AND *TRUST* OF MY AIDES.

AND WHEN YOU DISCOVERED THAT SOME OF THOSE AIDES HAD ENGAGED IN SMUGGLING HIGH-TECH ARMS TO THE TERRORIST ORGANIZATION KNOWN AS *D.M.T.*?

I WAS SHOCKED. DEEPLY SHOCKED. WE DO LIVE IN DECADENT TIMES.

I BELIEVE THAT YOUR OWN EXECUTIVE SECRETARY, ANGELICA GOODWIN, WAS A PART OF THIS CONSPIRACY?

TRUE. I WAS VIRTUALLY A *PRISONER* OF THE WOMAN'S CUNNING.

I COULD HAVE BEEN *KILLED* MYSELF, IF IT HADN'T BEEN FOR THE COURAGE OF DAVOOD NASSUR.

AND IT WAS GOODWIN, IN COMBINATION WITH THE D.M.T. WHO TRIED TO START THIS ANTI-*QURACI* *PURGE*--

--TO KILL DAVOOD NASSUR AND GET THE *META-POWER* BELT AWAY FROM HIM?

YES, AND NOW THAT THE BELT IS BURNED-OUT AND USE-LESS, I HOPE WE CAN ALL SEE HOW *FUTILE* THIS SORT OF SCHEME IS.

I THINK THIS HAS BEEN A LESSON IN HOW FRAGILE OUR SOCIAL CONTRACT IS AND HOW *VIGILANT* WE MUST BE IN PRESERVING THE RIGHTS OF *ALL* OUR CITIZENS.

MOST OF THE D.M.T. ESCAPED, UNFORTU-NATELY, BUT THEY WEREN'T THE WHOLE PROBLEM...

WE WERE ALL TOO EAGER TO SEE ALL *ARABS* AS TERRORISTS, AND TO ALLOW OUR *PREJUDICES* TO BE MANIPULATED--

--RATHER THAN EXTENDING THE HAND OF *BROTHERHOOD!*

THANK YOU, LEX LUTHOR.

WELL, HE'S *SLICK.* I ALMOST BELIEVE HIM.

YES. HE'S MANAGED TO *PAY* SOMEONE TO TAKE THE FALL FOR HIM *AGAIN.* NICE SPEECH, THOUGH.

HE EVEN *CALLED* ME AND OFFERED ME MY OLD JOB BACK, AS IF HE *HADN'T* BEEN TRYING TO *KILL* ME!

WELL, AS I TOLD YOU, SORAYA, THEY ALWAYS NEED GOOD SECRETARIES AT *THE PLANET.*

MR. WHITE TOLD ME YOU CAN INTERVIEW NEXT WEEK.

AND HOW ARE YOU FEELING, DAVOOD? WHAT DID THE SCIENTISTS *SAY* ABOUT YOUR POWERS?

WHEN THE BELT *FUSED,* I LOST *EVERYTHING.* I WAS AS WEAK AS A KITTEN. IF SUPERMAN HADN'T CAUGHT ME...

YOU KNOW, HE ISN'T A BAD GUY.

YOU SAVED THE *CITY,* DAVOOD. PEOPLE AREN'T GOING TO FORGET THAT. AND, WHO KNOWS, ONCE YOU'RE FULLY RESTED...

I KNOW. IT WAS *GREAT* BEING SO *POWERFUL.*

I DIDN'T MENTION TO THEM THAT I COULD STILL DO *THIS!*

SAY, YOUR POWERS *MAY* COME BACK AFTER ALL.

YEAH, BUT DON'T TELL *SUPERMAN.* THE *COMPETITION'D* JUST MAKE HIM *NERVOUS!*

MUM'S THE WORD, DAVOOD. MUM'S THE WORD!

end

Cover art by Kerry Gammill and John Nyberg.

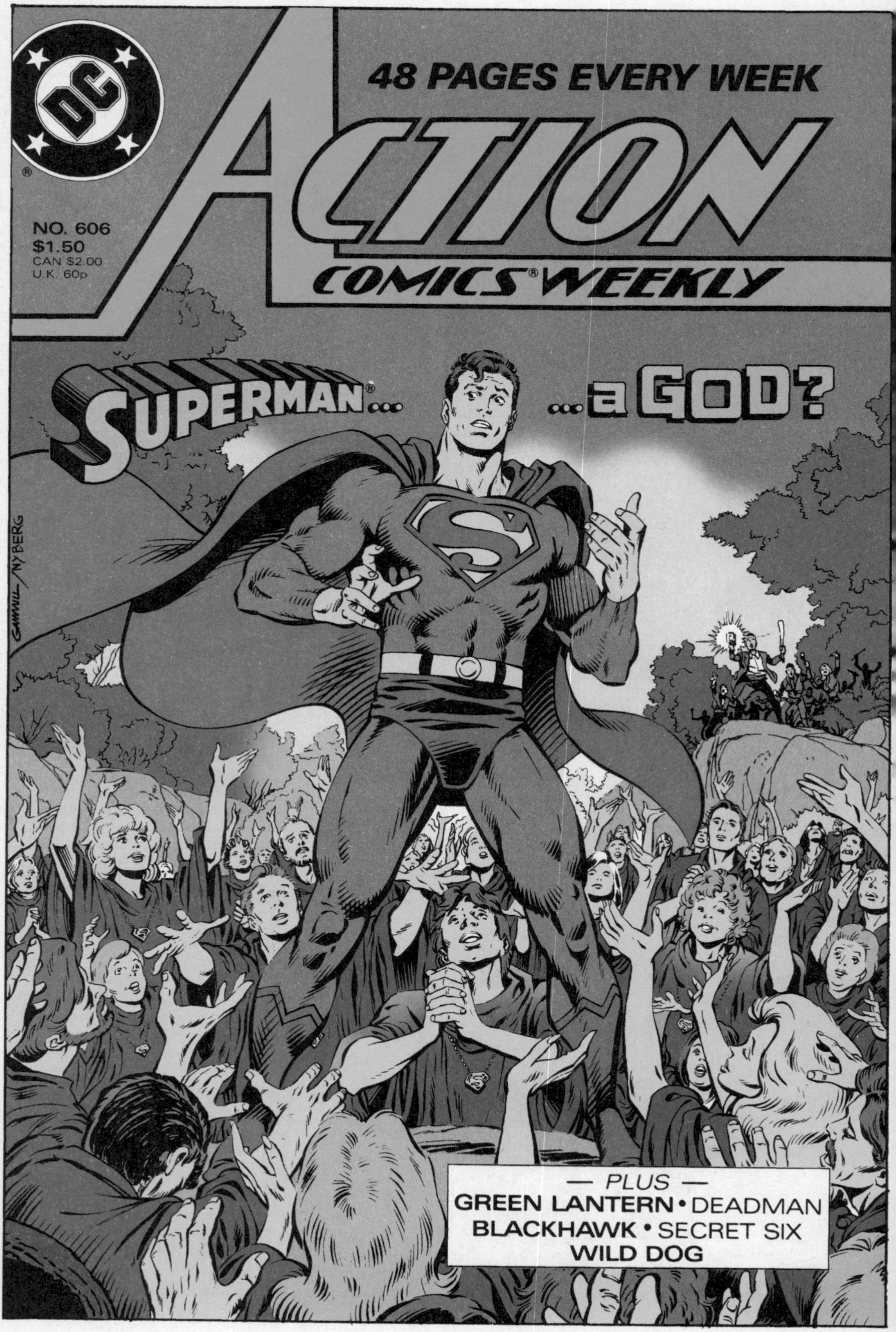
48 PAGES EVERY WEEK
ACTION
COMICS WEEKLY
NO. 606
$1.50
CAN $2.00
U.K. 60p
SUPERMAN... ...a GOD?
GAMMILL/NYBERG
— PLUS —
GREEN LANTERN • DEADMAN
BLACKHAWK • SECRET SIX
WILD DOG

Cover art by Alex Niño.

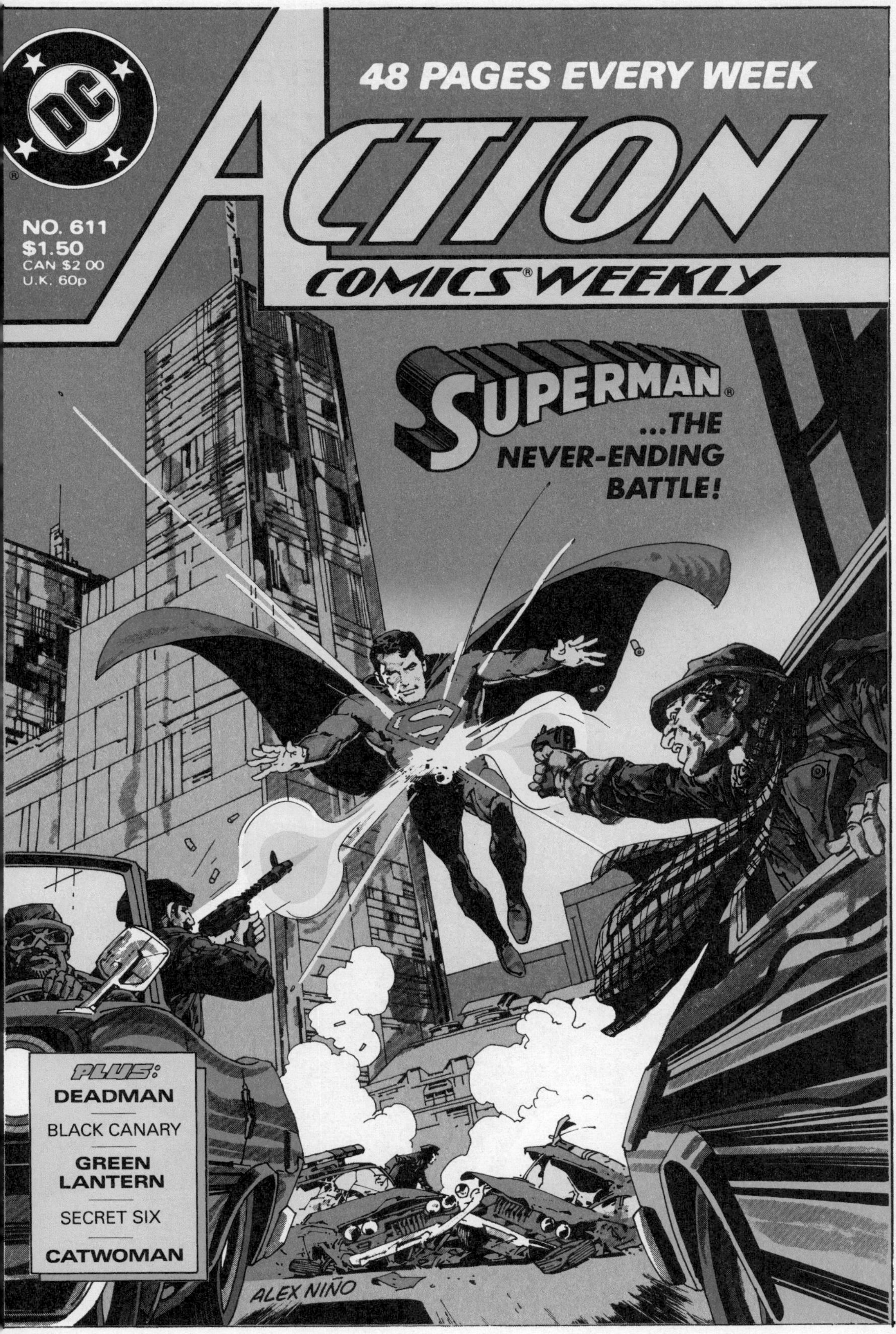

DC
48 PAGES EVERY WEEK
ACTION
COMICS WEEKLY
NO. 611
$1.50
CAN $2.00
U.K. 60p
SUPERMAN
...THE NEVER-ENDING BATTLE!
PLUS:
DEADMAN
BLACK CANARY
GREEN LANTERN
SECRET SIX
CATWOMAN
ALEX NIÑO

Cover art by Dean Motter.

48 PAGES EVERY WEEK

Action
COMICS WEEKLY

NO. 617
$1.50
CAN $2.00
U.K. 60p

SUPERMAN.

PLUS
BLACKHAWK · WILD DOG
GREEN LANTERN · NIGHTWING
AND **PHANTOM STRANGER**

48 PAGES--EVERY WEEK !

ACTION
COMICS WEEKLY

NO. 623
$1.50
CAN $2.00
U.K. 60p

SUPERMAN

PLUS:
GREEN
LANTERN
SECRET SIX
DEADMAN
PHANTOM
STRANGER
SHAZAM!

Cover art by John Severin.

Cover art by Murphy Anderson.

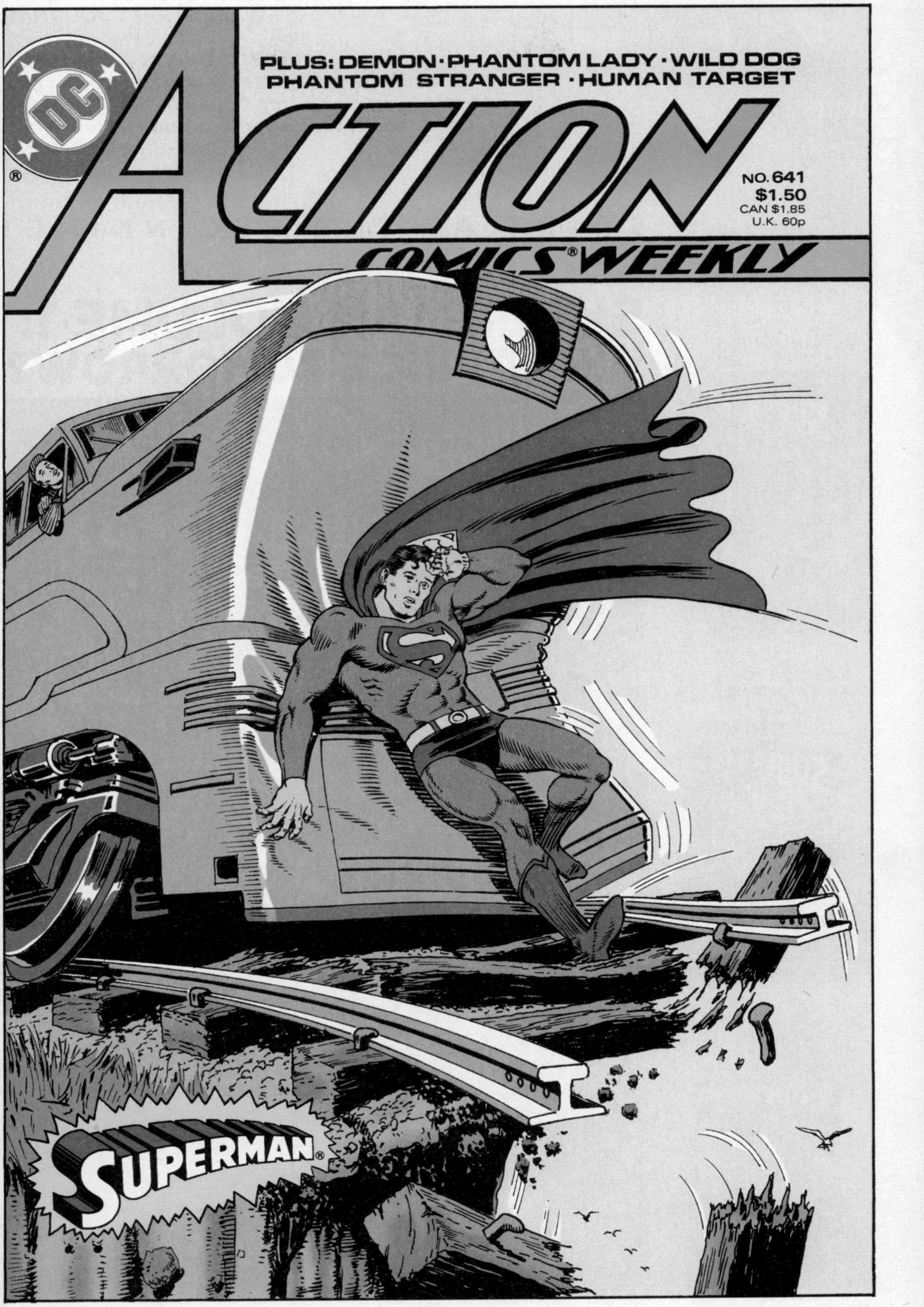
PLUS: DEMON · PHANTOM LADY · WILD DOG
PHANTOM STRANGER · HUMAN TARGET
DC
ACTION
NO. 641
$1.50
CAN $1.85
U.K. 60p
COMICS WEEKLY
SUPERMAN

DC COMICS™

"Superman is still super."
—WALL STREET JOURNAL

"The SUPERMAN world is also one now where fans new and old, young and not-so-young, can come to a common ground to talk about the superhero that started it all."
—CRAVE ONLINE

START AT THE BEGINNING!

SUPERMAN VOLUME 1: WHAT PRICE TOMORROW?

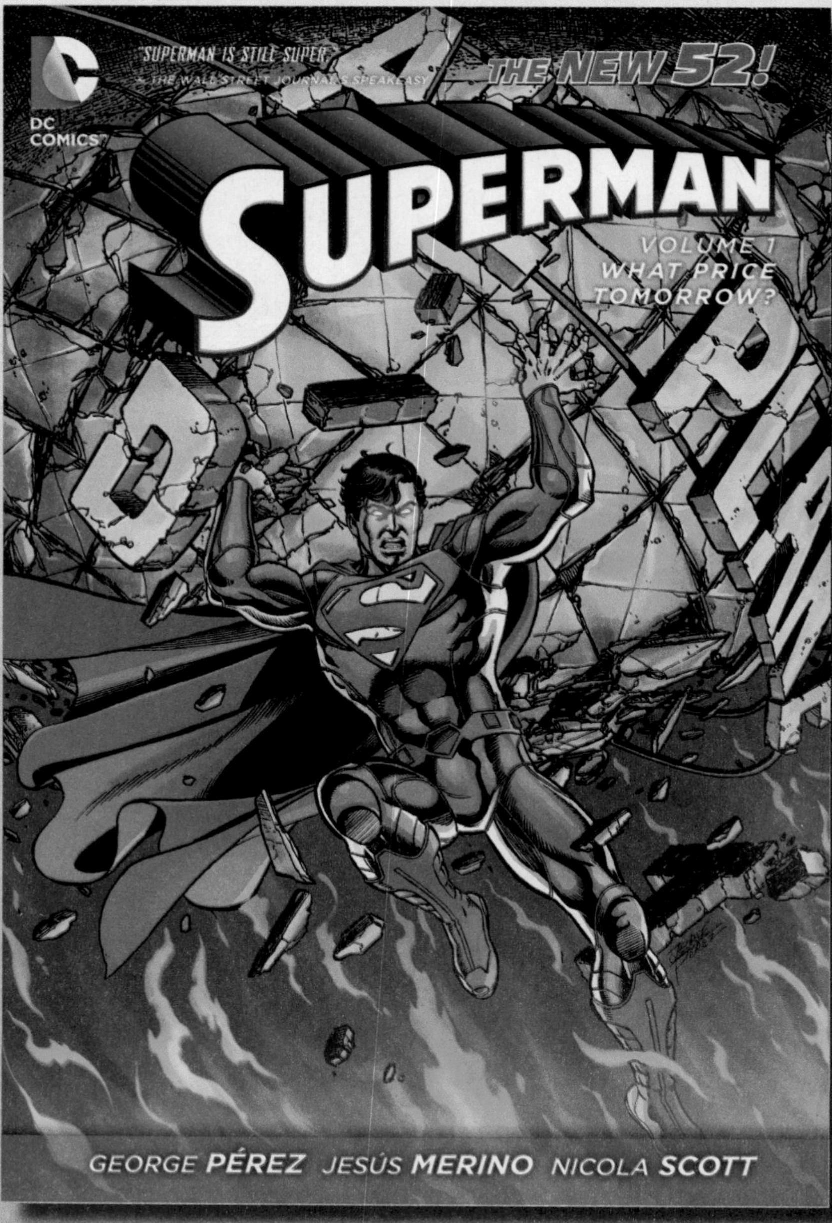
"SUPERMAN IS STILL SUPER."
THE NEW 52!
DC COMICS
SUPERMAN
VOLUME 1
WHAT PRICE TOMORROW?
GEORGE PÉREZ JESÚS MERINO NICOLA SCOTT

SUPERMAN VOL. 2: SECRETS & LIES

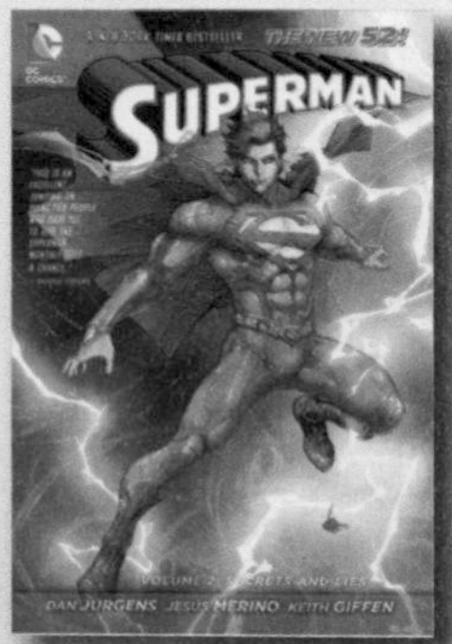
THE NEW 52!
SUPERMAN
DAN JURGENS JESUS MERINO KEITH GIFFEN

SUPERMAN VOL. 3: FURY AT WORLD'S END

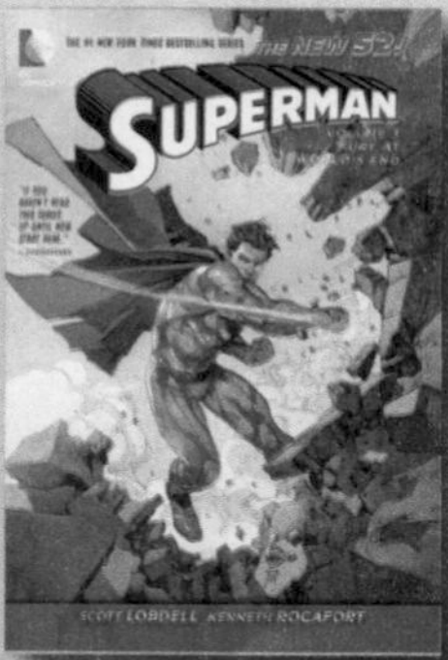
THE NEW 52!
SUPERMAN
SCOTT LOBDELL KENNETH ROCAFORT

SUPERMAN: H'EL ON EARTH

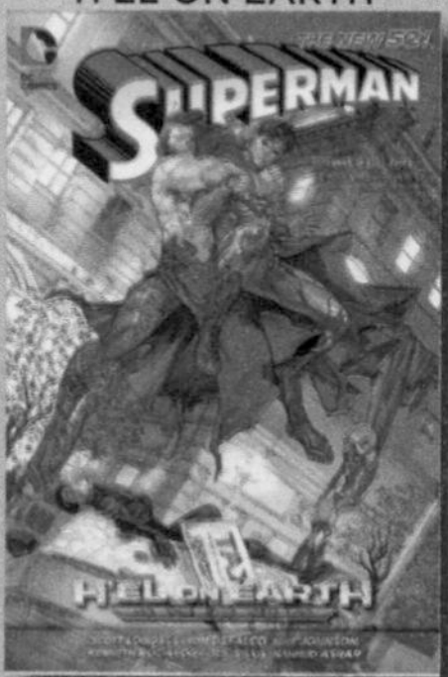
THE NEW 52!
SUPERMAN
H'EL ON EARTH

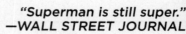

FROM THE CREATOR OF *300* and *SIN CITY*

FRANK MILLER
with KLAUS JANSON

BATMAN: THE DARK KNIGHT STRIKES AGAIN

BATMAN: YEAR ONE DELUXE EDITION

with DAVID MAZZUCCHELLI

ALL-STAR BATMAN & ROBIN, THE BOY WONDER VOL. 1

with JIM LEE

BATMAN: THE DARK KNIGHT RETURNS

FRANK MILLER

with KLAUS JANSON and LYNN VARLEY

If we do not plant knowledge
when young, it will give us no shade
when we are old.
—*Lord Chesterfield*

Nowhere can man find a
quieter or more untroubled retreat
than in his own soul.
—*Marcus Aurelius*

Every action of our lives
touches on some chord that
will vibrate in eternity.
—*Edwin Hubbel Chapin*

What is it about grandparents that is so lovely?
I'd like to say that grandparents are God's gifts to children.
And if they can but see, hear, and feel what these people
have to give, they can mature at a fast rate.
—*Bill Cosby*

Heaven never helps
the man who will not act.
—*Sophocles*

A child needs a grandparent, anybody's grandparent,
to grow a little more securely into an unfamiliar world.
—*Charles and Ann Morse*

The poor man is not
he who is without a cent,
but he who is without a dream.
—*Harry Kemp*

Ask and it will be given to you;
seek and you will find;
Knock and the door will be opened to you.
—*Bible, Matthew 7:7*

A journey of a thousand miles begins
with a single step.
—*Confucius*

The Growing Field series was inspired by, and written in memory of,
my colleague, mentor, and friend Jason Dahl —
the Captain of Flight 93 that crashed in Pennsylvania on September 11, 2001.
May your voice — and your leadership message — live on forever!

The Growing Field series is dedicated to my sister Michele.
You believed in me and this series long before I did...
with a world of love and thanks.

Field of Dreams *is dedicated to every grandparent who has passed down*
stories, values, traditions, and love. Especially to...
Leo & Edna and George & Thelma: For the grandparents you have been to me.
Thomas & Sandy and Luther & Roberta: For the grandparents you are to my children.

— Mark Hoog

Thanks to my inspiring family and friends for the seeds of
encouragement you planted within my Field of Dreams.

— Mark Wayne Adams

A portion of all Growing Field proceeds are donated to the
Children's Leadership Institute for the promotion of youth character education.
A portion of all Growing Field proceeds are donated to the Jason Dahl Scholarship Fund.

Field of Dreams

A Growing Field Adventure

Written by Mark E. Hoog

Illustrated by Mark Wayne Adams

For information regarding permissions, contact Growing Field Books at:

Growing Field Books
2012 Pacific Ct.
Ft. Collins, CO 80528

Written by Mark E. Hoog. Illustrated and designed by Mark W. Adams. Edited by Jennifer Thomas.

Publisher's Cataloging-in-Publication
(Provided by Quality Books, Inc.)

Hoog, Mark E.
Field of dreams : a growing field adventure /
written by Mark E. Hoog ; illustrated by Mark W. Adams.
-- 1st ed.
p. cm.

SUMMARY:
In the magical Growing Field two young farmers discover
their own field of dreams and learn to grow their own seeds of success.

LCCN 2009920143
ISBN-13: 978-0-9770391-3-5
ISBN-10: 0-9770391-3-7

1. Success--Juvenile fiction. 2. Self-esteem--
Juvenile fiction. 3. Self-actualization (Psychology)--
Juvenile fiction. [1. Success--Fiction. 2. Self-esteem
--Fiction. 3. Self-actualization (Psychology)--Fiction.
4. Gardening--Fiction. 5. Stories in rhyme.]
I. Adams, Mark Wayne, 1971- ill. II. Title.

PZ8.3.H7625Fi 2009
[E]
QBI09-200012

Printed in China / August 2009

Growing Field Books
Where children go to grow! ™

"*There is a time in every man's education when he arrives at the conviction that envy is ignorance…that though the wide universe is full of good, no kernel of nourishing corn can come to him but through his toil bestowed on that plot of ground which is given to him to till.*"

— Ralph Waldo Emerson

Spectacular children live in the magical town of Walden.

Some are tall, some short. Some have light hair and others dark.
Some are big, others small. Some wear glasses and others do not.
The children in Walden are just like you!

2

So, you may ask, what makes these children so spectacular?

The answer is found in the questions they ask and the answers they discover in a magical place called the *Growing Field*.

It is here where the wise sage *Nightingale* mysteriously appears to share ideas about making their dreams in life come true.

3

Nightingale appears in many forms, to creatively show Walden children how to live life without limit.

Some say *Nightingale's* ideas can be used forever!

The best part: the children from Walden love to share their *Growing Field* discoveries with you.

4

Today was another special day in Walden
as Dusty looked out over her grandparents' farm.

Through the years, Dusty had heard stories of a *Field of Dreams*,
where seeds for the future are planted and grown.

5

Today Dusty found herself asking, "What if *I* could visit the *Field of Dreams* and plant the seeds for *my* future? What would I wish for? What could I achieve?"

Seeing her grandparents approach with a thick family photo album, Dusty knew her favorite Walden tradition was about to begin: Story time!

"When I was your age," Grandpa began, "I planted 'Seeds of Success' in a magical place called the *Field of Dreams*."

7

"Stop now, Grandpa!" laughed Grandma, having heard this tale many times.
"Everyone knows the *Field of Dreams* disappeared long ago."

Meanwhile, she quietly slipped a photo from the album into Dusty's pocket.
She and Grandpa tangled their fingers with Dusty's, and they all closed their eyes.

8

Dusty's eyes opened to the most unusual sight…

There in a truck, she couldn't believe what she saw:
A pot-bellied gopher, chewing a long piece of straw.
Looking at Dusty, the gopher smiled and said, "Hi."
With a wink and a wave, he kept driving right by.

Off her grandparents' porch
                    Dusty decided to slide;
She ran to the truck
                    and jumped in for a ride.

9

"Maybe now," Dusty thought, "I'll make my magical find."
She could picture the field perfectly, inside her mind.

But with her eyes shut, she missed, on the side of a tree,
the sign with the words she'd waited her whole life to see.

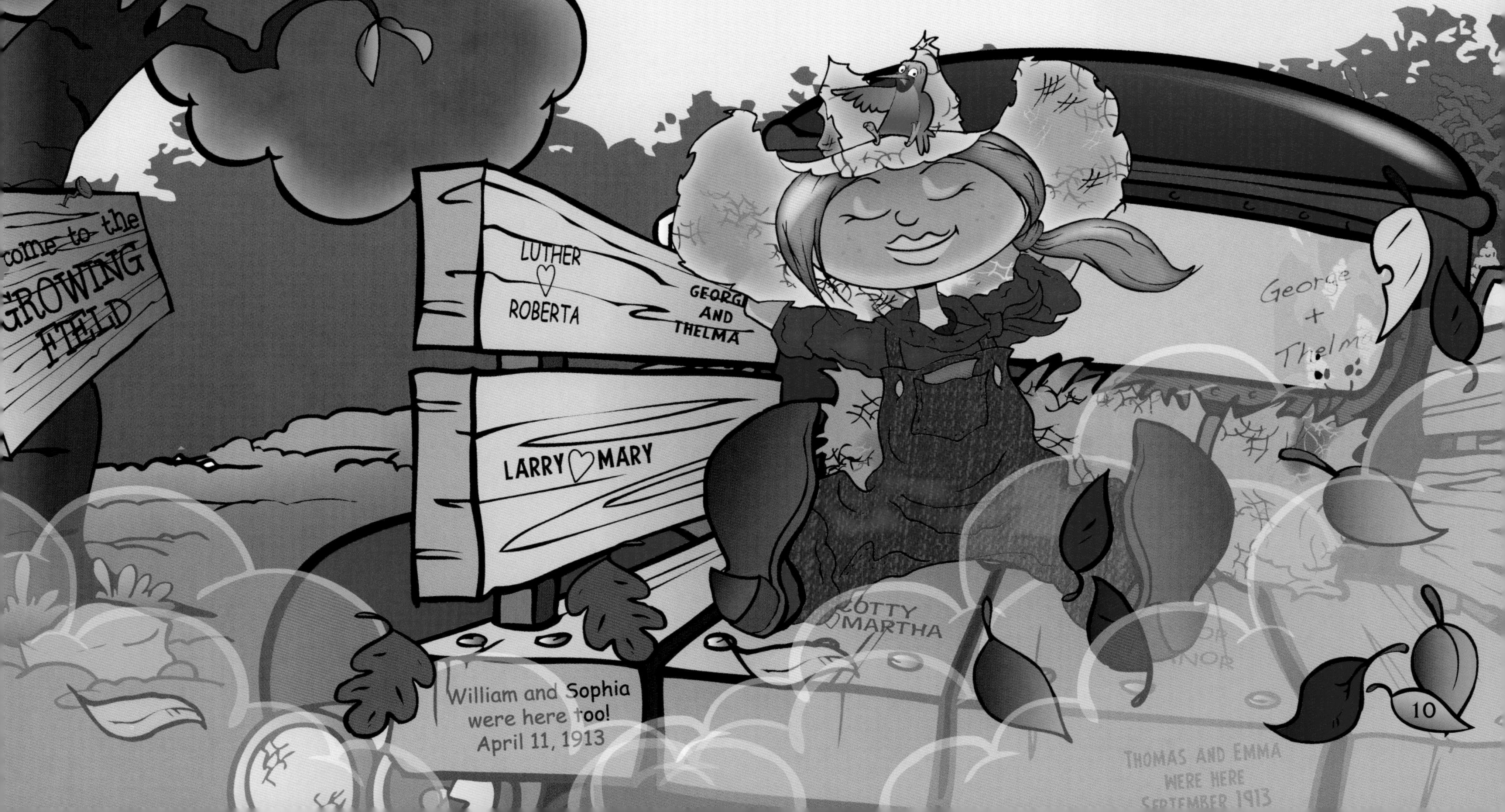
come to the
GROWING
FIELD
LUTHER ♡ ROBERTA
GEORG AND THELMA
LARRY ♡ MARY
George + Thelm
William and Sophia
were here too!
April 11, 1913
THOMAS AND EMMA
WERE HERE

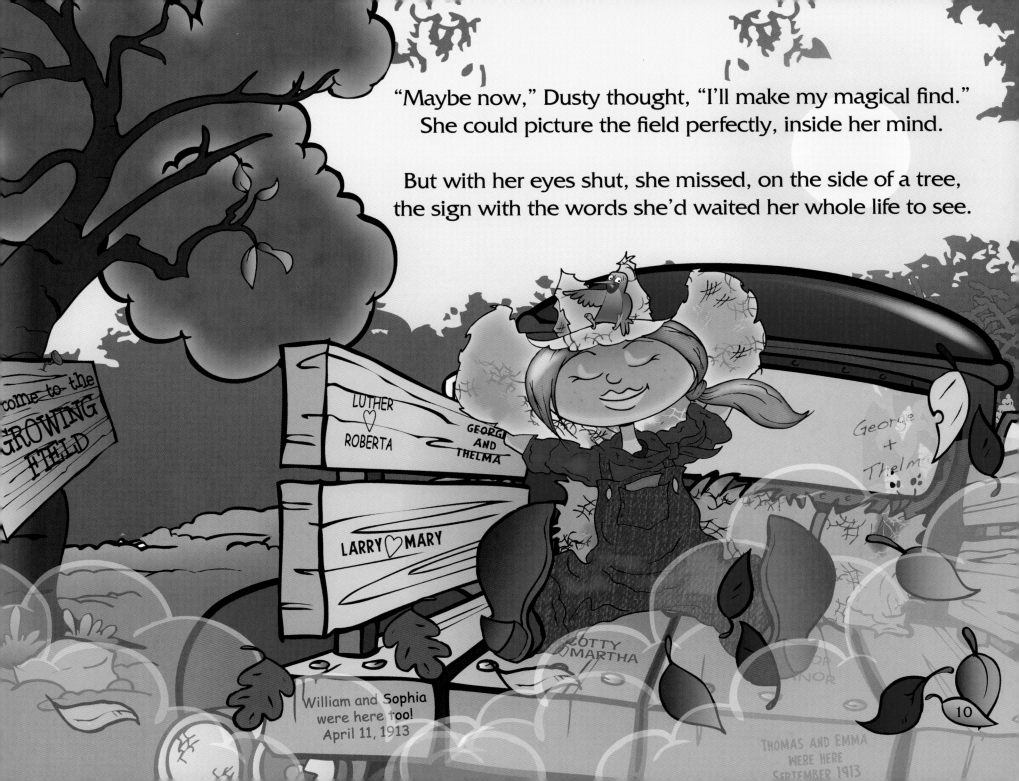

"Mr. Gopher," said Dusty. "I have a question today.
I'm looking for the *Field of Dreams*. Can you show me the way?
For I see on your truck, written here on the side,
that you know where it is. Would you give me a ride?"

"The name's Gus," smiled the gopher, "and I'll be happy to show.
But I think there is something that, first, you must know.
In that field, there is nothing left to be found,
except dirt with some weeds growing up from the ground."

"Long ago," Gus explained, "I went with one wish to make.
It never came true, though—there was some sort of mistake.
But of course I will show you. In fact, here's a secret I'll share:
We arrived a moment ago. We are already there!"

12

The field, Dusty saw, had been ignored for many years.
Looking over the landscape, she couldn't hold back her tears.

13

"Nothing magical here," said Gus. "Nothing special to be found.
Just cups, trash, and wrappers that have blown all around—
and an old rusty wagon melted into the ground."

"I can't believe it!" cried Dusty. "I'd hoped the stories were wrong.
But I can see we're too late: The *Field of Dreams* is already gone."

14

"But now that we're here," Dusty said. "I think we should stay.
Let's pretend the field is alive, and make a wish anyway."

"I bet it won't work," said Gus, climbing up on his truck.
"My wishes never come true—I seem to have the worst luck."

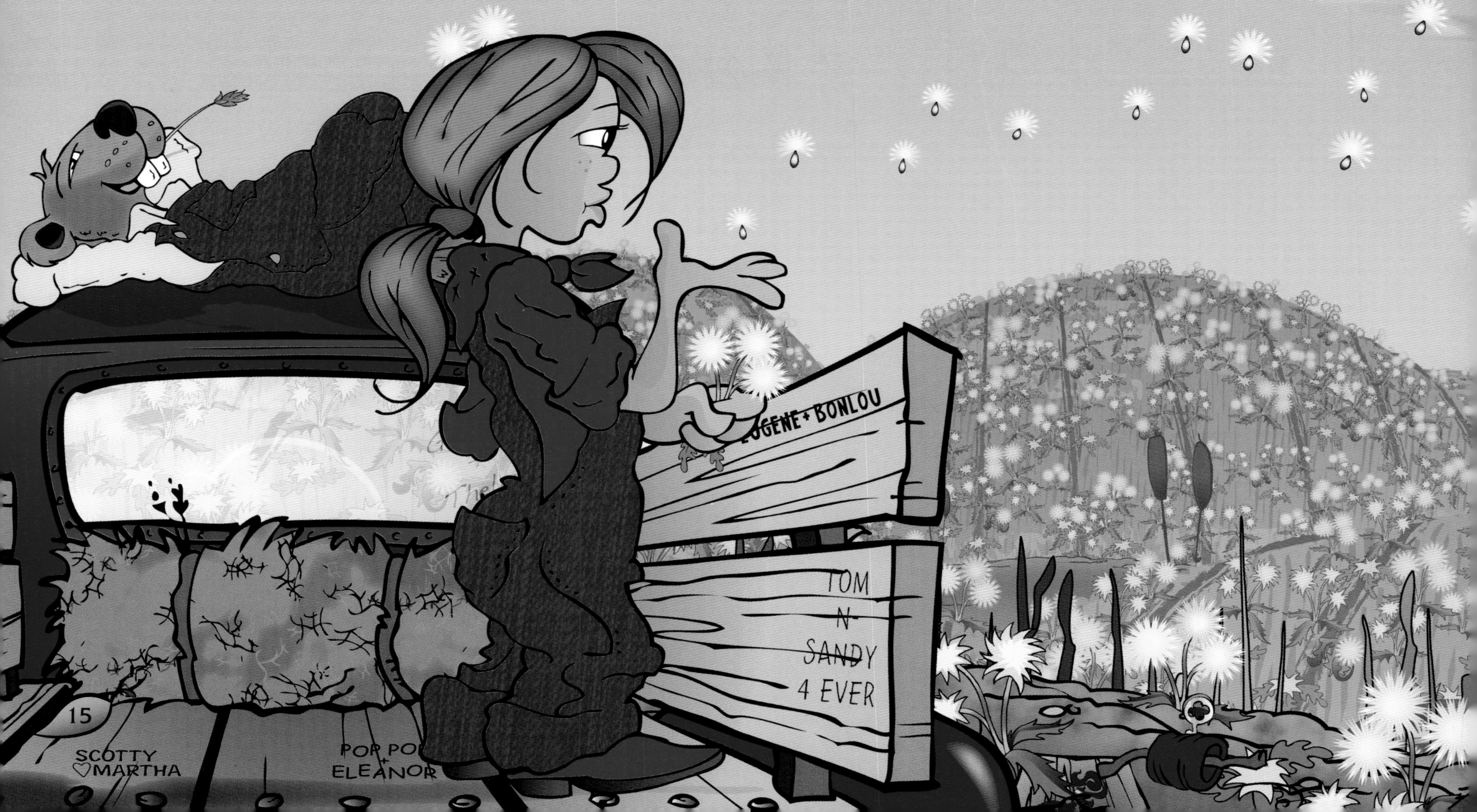
UGENE + BONLOU
TOM N SANDY 4 EVER
SCOTTY ♡MARTHA
POP POP + ELEANOR

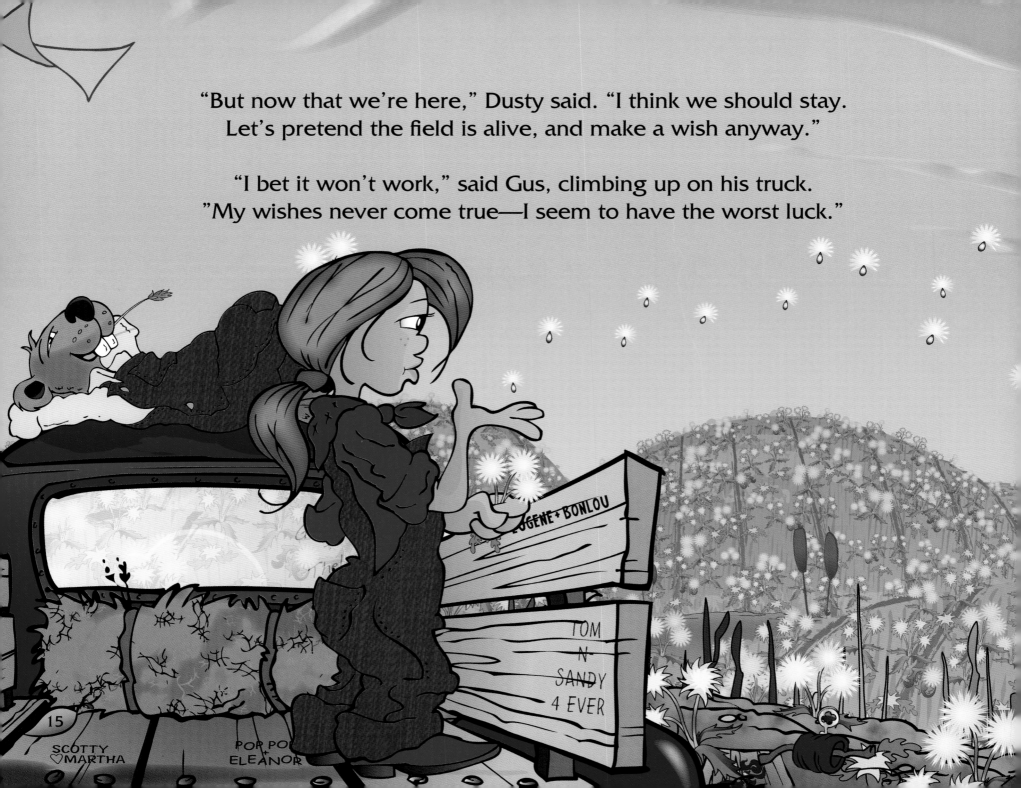

"You must learn to wish," declared Dusty, "in just the right way.
Tell yourself all that is possible with everything that you say.
Find the reasons you can, and all of the reasons you should.
Most importantly, say my grandparents, find the reasons you could."

Gus smiled in wonder. "Could that really be true?
If so," he remarked, "that would be so easy to do."

16

"So, what did you wish for?" asked Dusty.
"What dream to come true?"
"Bringing back this field," Gus replied,
"is what I want *most* to do."

Dusty smiled and she said:
"Well, that is now my wish, too.
Let's bring this *Field of Dreams* back to life,
just for you."

17

From the legends, Dusty knew, that *Nightingale* must be found.
"We need you," whispered Dusty, but *Nightingale* was nowhere around.

Still, Dusty promised Gus that her word she would keep.
And with the moon watching over them, both drifted to sleep.

Come morning, as the pair brushed off the night,
they saw the old rusty wagon holding a wonderful sight.

"Your dreams will come true!" Dusty exclaimed to Gus.
"Look at all these seed packets, here just for us!"

"*Seeds of Success:*" Dusty read, "*For anything one could possibly dream.*
There must be a gazillion—at least that's what it seems.
The directions say we must begin right away.
Tomorrow's too late; we must start planting today."

The two went to work, and began to laugh, dance, and sing
as they started to imagine what each seed would bring.

They didn't want to wait even one second more
to see what the *Field of Dreams* had in store.

As they opened each packet, they leapt all around,
making sure that each seed found a place in the ground.

At long last they finished—each seed had been sown.
They sat down and waited for their dreams to be grown.

22

They sat and they stared—believing they had no more to do.
For a long time they waited, but still nothing grew.

"Is it the fault of the seeds?" wondered Gus.
"Is this the wrong piece of ground?"

"Maybe," said Dusty,
"the secret to the field has still not been found."

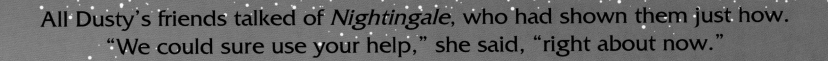

All Dusty's friends talked of *Nightingale*, who had shown them just how.
"We could sure use your help," she said, "right about now."

That night as the stars put on their shimmering show,
they both thought about how they could make their dreams grow.

"My grandparents say, that for dreams to come true,
I must believe in what's possible and *work* to make it come true.
'Do a little each day' is what they say wins the race."
Dusty's grandparents' picture brought a smile to her face.

24

In the morning, the moonlight gave way to the sun;
for two tired farmers, a new day had begun.

"If dreams can't come true," Dusty said, "then what are they for?
We need you now, *Nightingale*, just send one answer more."

Then she looked in the wagon—"Look here, Gus!" she yelled.
For, some tools for planting were what it now held.

25

Her grandparents had told her of a move all must make.
Dusty smiled as she realized: They had made a mistake.
"We must get to work!" she explained.
"It's the next step we must take."

26

With so much to be done, neither took a single break.
Dusty pulled weeds while Gus worked with the rake.

They toiled into the night and on through the week,
both working their hardest, barely taking time to speak.

Dusty and Gus worked straight through the fall,
through the wind and the seasons—
they worked through it all.

28

Month after month, missing not a single thing—
they worked till fall became winter…

...and winter again became spring!

With evening approaching, the sun starting to fade,
they pulled the last weed together,
and one last wish was made.

SEEDS OF
SUCCESS

31

Standing next to his friend, Gus proclaimed aloud:
"Of our work and this field we both can be proud."

Dusty believed in her heart, she somehow just knew,
Nightingale would answer and would once more come through.

SEEDS OF
GREATNESS

Seeds of
Inspiration

OLD TIME
DREAMS

The field now perfect, two farmers knelt to the ground.
They bowed and gave thanks for the seeds they had found.

Softly, the rain began to fall down.

Pouring down through the night, it washed the old wagon clean,
and by the light of the moon, *Nightingale's* name was now seen.

As had happened before, with Walden friends that she knew,
Dusty knew it was *her* turn to learn to make dreams come true.

34

Retrieving her grandparents' picture once more,
Dusty saw writing she'd not noticed before.

In her grandmother's hand were simple words to be read.
Through the tears in her eyes, she recited all that it said:

*Many spend their whole life waiting to be shown
"Seeds of Success" and a "Field of Dreams" of their own.*

*Many make wishes and just hope for the best,
while others have faith and put themselves to the test.*

*We are all given the sun, the soil, and the seed;
but we grow our own garden—
hard work is all we need.*

"Gus, your Seeds of Success will grow one by one,
just as soon as the soil is touched by the sun!"

With a smile, Dusty picked up the rake once again
and placed the tool gently in the hand of her friend.

"Help all *Growing Field* gardeners grow *their* Seeds of Success.
Teach them to believe, to work hard, and always give it their best.

Life's greatest secret with the world you must share:

36

With goals and hard work, Seeds of Success can grow...

OLD TIME DREAMS

37

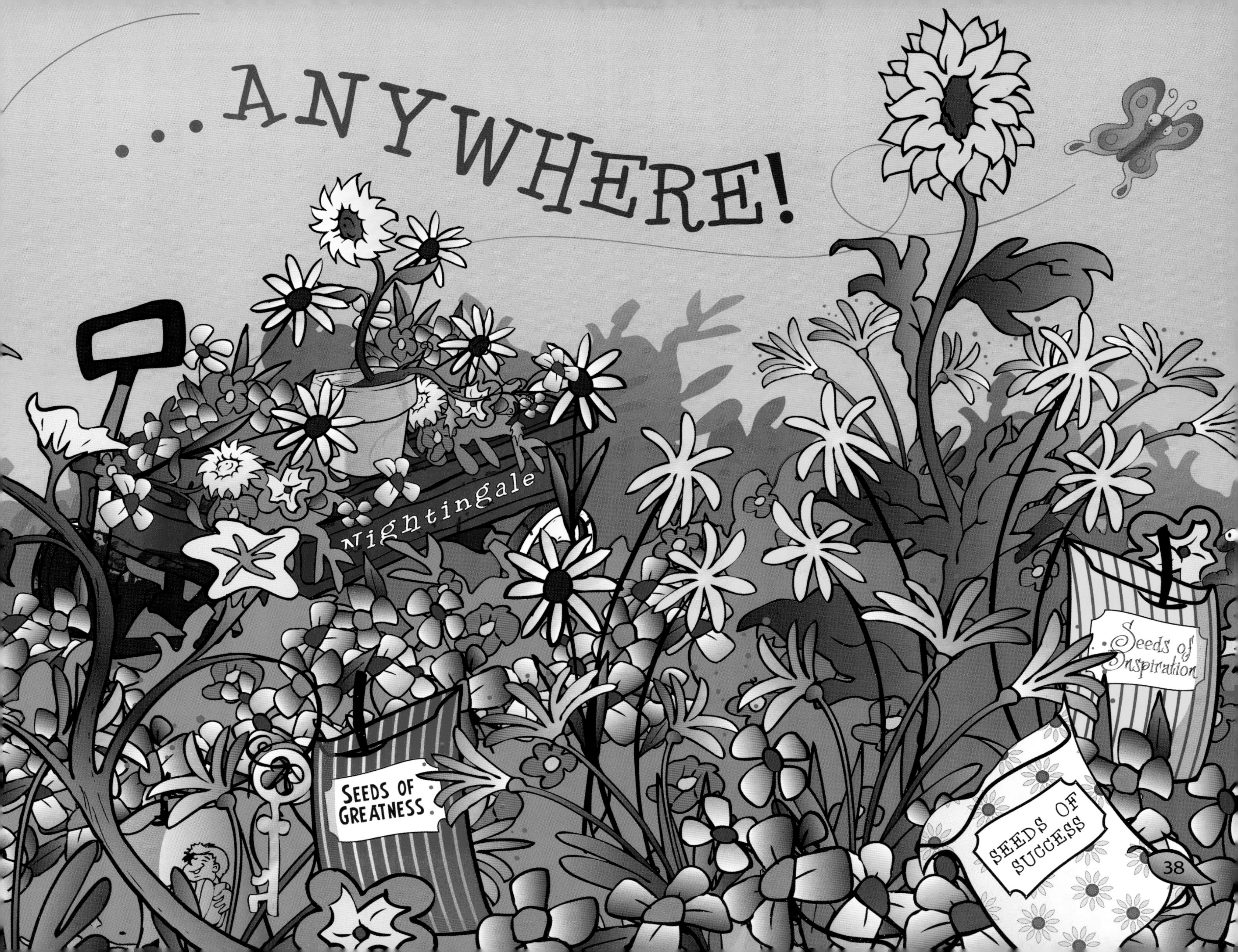

...ANYWHERE!
Nightingale
Seeds of Inspiration
SEEDS OF GREATNESS
SEEDS OF SUCCESS

"Share your *Field of Dreams*, Gus. Invite all to see:
With our Seeds of Success, we can be *anything* we choose to be!"

39

"Thank you, Dusty," said Gus, "for our adventure together.
All you have taught me has changed my life forever."

Picking some flowers, Dusty said, "I must go!
I must find my grandparents—
there's something they've just got to know."

40

"I did it!" Dusty told them. "Because of what you both taught me, I worked hard and planted my own Seeds of Success in the *Field of Dreams.* I can't thank you enough for your love, guidance, and stories— you mean the world to me!" Her grandparents smiled at her proudly.

"Grandma and Grandpa," asked Dusty, "did *your* 'Seeds' ever come true?" "Yes, dear," they said, hugging her, "today they grew inside of you!"

41

"We almost forgot, Dusty!" said Grandpa.
"This is for you to share with your friends back in Walden."

Dusty opened a rickety old crate to find a shiny new wagon!
She opened the single seed packet lying inside it
and found a special note:

Always believe in your
Field of Dreams! Your
goals and hard work will
make all your Seeds of
Success bloom.

I love you, little farmer!
Nightingale

42

Discussion Seeds for *Field of Dreams*

Field of Dreams teaches children that life responds not when they "want" or "wish," but instead, when they *create* their vision, *courageously* take the first step toward realizing that vision, and *commit* to all the steps required to *complete* the task at hand.

Leaders understand that a successful harvest in the spring is the result of a yearly plan, broken down into months, weeks, and days. Help your child develop the disciplines needed to become an effective life farmer, by teaching the concept of *sowing and reaping*.

Questions to ask your son or daughter:

- If you could grow your own Seeds of Success, what seeds would you plant?
  Dream with your child about the future.

- What can you do *today* to help that seed grow? What will your first step be?
  Identify the disciplines necessary to pursue that dream.

- What will your *Field of Dreams* look like when you are finished?
  Make sure your son knows how to close his eyes and visualize his dreams. Make sure your daughter understands the importance of then opening her eyes and working to make her dreams come true.

Tell your daughter you believe in her unique Seeds of Success! Tell your son you think his *Field of Dreams* is spectacular. It's never too early to teach children about the seasons of life and for them to begin cultivating their own incredible *Field of Dreams*!

Start today—don't delay!